WAR
TO BE
ONE

LEVI O. KEIDEL
WAR TO BE ONE

ZONDERVAN PUBLISHING HOUSE
OF THE ZONDERVAN CORPORATION
GRAND RAPIDS, MICHIGAN 49506

WAR TO BE ONE
© 1977 by The Zondervan Corporation
Grand Rapids, Michigan

Library of Congress Cataloging in Publication Data

Keidel, Levi O
    War to be one.

    1. Missions—Zaire.   2. Mennonites—Missions.
3. Zaire—History—Civil War, 1960-1965.   I. Title.
BV3625.C6K4   266'.9'70924 [B]   77-6302

Cloth   ISBN 0-310-35370-X
Paper   ISBN 0-310-35371-8

Photographs are courtesy of:
    Archie Graber's personal files
    African Inter-Mennonite Mission *(AIMM)*
    Mennonite Central Committee, Akron, Pennsylvania *(MCC)*
    World Council of Churches, Geneva, Switzerland *(WCC)*

Printed in the United States of America.

To the Christians of Zaire,
whose courage before great obstacles
and patience in deep suffering
are an enduring inspiration
to us who have known so little hardship

Contents

Acknowledgments

The Commission on Overseas Mission of the General Conference Mennonite Church provided financial support for my wife and me beyond the end of our regular furlough to allow me to give full time to this project.

Dr. Miriam Fackler trenchantly and constructively criticized the initial draft.

Connie Wickert and Donna Lehman typed the final manuscript.

My wife, Eudene, provided constant encouragement during nine months of writing.

Together, their help has made it possible for me to share with others what I feel to be a powerful human drama.

WAR
TO BE
ONE

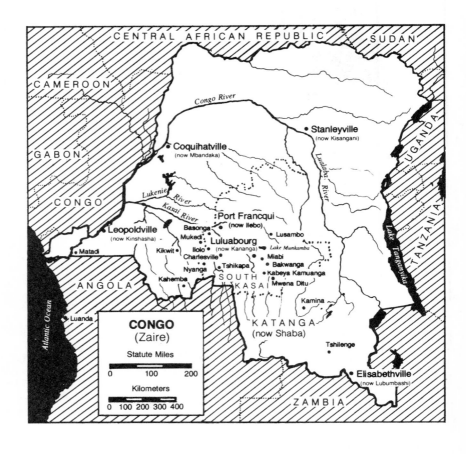

CENTRAL AFRICAN REPUBLIC

SUDAN

CAMEROON

GABON

CONGO

Congo River

• Stanleyville
(now Kisangani)

Lualaba River

UGANDA

• Coquihatville
(now Mbandaka)

Lukenie River

Kasai River

Port Francqui
(now Ilebo)

Basonga

• Lusambo

Mukedi

• Luluabourg
(now Kananga)

Lake Munkamba

TANZANIA

Lake Tanganyika

Leopoldville
(now Kinshasha)

Kikwit •

Ilolo •

Charlesville •

Nyanga

• Miabi
• Bakwanga

• Kabeya Kamuanga
Mwena Ditu

• Matadi

Tshikapa •

SOUTH
KASAI

Kahemba •

Kamina
•

ANGOLA

• Luanda

Atlantic Ocean

KATANGA
(now Shaba)

Tshilenge
•

• Elisabethville
(now Lubumbashi)

CONGO
(Zaire)

Statute Miles

0   100   200

Kilometers

0   100 200 300 400

ZAMBIA

Part 1

... A Growing Plant ...

1

... Flight for Life ...

THE OLD BLACK pastor sat at the dining room table in a brick dwelling left vacant by missionaries. His wife was putting dishes into a cupboard nearby; his teenage son slouched forlornly in a wooden armchair. Suddenly the man tensed his long, slender frame, turned his ear toward the open window, and listened with concentration that furrowed his brow. His wife paused.

What's that noise about?'' she asked.

The sound of angry voices was building to a crescendo. It was as he had feared. Such sounds had become familiar these days. The pastor felt the muscles of his body tighten like those of an animal whose life is threatened. He had occupied this house to defuse crisis. Now crisis threatened again. His body, so many times numbed by crises, now responded merely with a feeling of weariness.

"It is the noise of young men who are looking for war," he answered. "They're coming down the path."

The date: early July 1961. The place: a large, deserted mission station on the hill slope of a tiny inland river port then known as Charlesville, Congo. The nation was one year old. It was a tumultuous era — when political opportunists carved out their kingdoms, proclaimed national autonomy, and stationed privately conscripted armies to defend their borders; when intertribal wars waged unchecked, disintegrating social order; when national leaders conducted fruitless parleys and waged savage wars in an effort to impose central authority; and when United Nations troops intervened to reduce the possibility of

13

interference by the world's great powers sparking a global conflagration. The tribal confrontation we are about to witness is a microcosm of a malady of nationwide scale.

The old man arose, picked up his chair, and with quiet resolution walked out the front door of the mission house onto the veranda. It was shaded by a corrugated iron roof and fronted with a row of square brick columns. He set down the chair and lifted his eyes to a scene electric with tension: some thirty anger-frenzied Bakuba warriors were crowding toward his doorstep. Their faces and bare torsos, streaked with sweat, gleamed black in the midday sun. They gripped in their hands spears and broad-bladed machetes, and carried around their necks the amulets of war.

He shouted a greeting to arrest their attention.

"Life to you!"

"Uhhh," a few responded disgruntedly. He sat down and viewed the scene beneath the rank overgrowth of an old bougainvillea vine, which crowned the front of the veranda, its gay lavender blossoms seeming to protest that things shouldn't be this way. The mob grew quiet. He spoke.

"What is your problem?"

"The time has come for you to get out of our country and return to your fatherland," one youth shouted brazenly.

"That's right," others chimed in. "We're driving you out today." They jabbed with their weapons for emphasis. The words were supported with jerky nods and a rumble of surly remarks. The pastor paused until the noise subsided, then spoke.

"My friends, I have sat here with you for forty years; when your fathers were but infants, I was already here. My nine children were born and raised among you. Why is it you want to chase me out today?"

"Get out!" they shouted. Then came a tumult of threats.

"Tie your things together and begin your journey!"

"If you refuse, today we're spilling your blood onto the ground!"

"My countrymen, I do not refuse to go. But intelligent people do not kill a man for nothing. For years following one another, I taught your parents in Bible school. I've baptized. I've preached. I've eaten at your tables. I've sat at your mournings. Wherever I walked among the tribes of this region, people would nod and say, 'There goes our pastor,

Matthew Kazadi.'[1] Why are you angry with me now? Are you saying today that I have become a bad person? I am not disrespecting your word. But for what reason are you driving me away?''

The warriors looked at each other calculating how to respond. Then one spoke.

''Don't you know we've entered political independence? What accounts for all these tribal wars? Don't you know it's time for every tribe to return to the land from which it came? Your great Baluba chief Kalonji[2] has himself heralded the message. We heard it on the radio. He is establishing his own kingdom in South Kasai; he is calling all his people to return to help him build it. Why don't you want to obey your chief and go?''

''We know why he doesn't want to go,'' said another. ''When the missionaries left, they put the keys to their homes and the mission buildings into the hands of Kazadi. It is as people tell us. He and his Baluba people plan to ransack the missionaries' houses and flee with their things, leaving us with empty hands.''

Suddenly Kazadi heard a commotion over his right shoulder, coming from around the corner of the house.

''You are lying!'' someone shouted.

''Don't touch the body of that pastor. If you do, we fight,'' ordered others.

A large group of his own Baluba tribesmen was rapidly converging from behind the house. They moved toward confrontation.

''So you're going to drive us out today?'' vanguards of the group challenged. ''Come on. Let's see.''

Kazadi stood quickly and extended his arms across a neglected brick flower box which fronted the veranda.

''Stand where you are,'' he ordered firmly. ''Don't touch one another. There is no reason to fight. Go call your chiefs; bring them here; we will talk and settle this matter.''

He moved to the top step, affirming his command. The sun caught the creases in his forehead and cast a deep shadow across his lean cheek. Gradually the tribesmen dispersed.

Then he sat down on the chair to ponder. What should he do? When he first arrived here as a schoolboy in 1916, who could have imagined

[1]Pronounced Kah-zah-dee
[2]Kah-loh-nshee

such a day as this? From that time, he cast his lot with the missionaries. He studied their Book. He came to believe its message. He tried to live by it. He and others spent their lives teaching it. A church of some twenty thousand believers in a dozen far-flung tribes emerged. He was elected its spiritual leader. It grew in strength and maturity. The Africa Inter-Mennonite Mission (AIMM), which had begun the work, sent a delegation from the States to draw up procedures for transferring leadership responsibility to African nationals.

Then came political independence just a year ago. The army mutinied. Missionaries left. Their work was suspended. Fear and mistrust spread like a plague and festered into war. His own fields and his coffee plantation, about to bear its first long-awaited harvest, were burned; his home was looted; the area was occupied by an enemy tribe. Church plans were jettisoned. More and more, Christians were now receding into hostile, fearful tribal enclaves. Traveling between the groups was growing increasingly dangerous. How could so much have happened in a single year?

Where were the missionaries who had involved him in all of this? Where was the one with whom he had worked hardest, Archie Graber, whom tribesmen had named "Lutonga"?[3] This house, which Kazadi had occupied since the day evacuating missionaries had left him in charge of their things, had for years been the home of Lutonga. Most of the brick buildings that made up the station complex had been constructed by Lutonga. True, a few missionaries had returned to safer areas, but none had returned to Charlesville. Why should the brunt of all these events fall upon him?

He was witnessing the unbelievable. The work of forty years was crumbling before his eyes. He was helpless to prevent it. His further presence would only hasten the process and inevitably entangle him and his people. Local tribesmen were right. It was time for him to leave.

But this was not a good time to travel. The area which separated him from the Baluba homeland in South Kasai, 250 miles to the east, was inhabited by Lulua, tribesmen who had once held the Baluba as slaves, and who were now their belligerent enemies. If he and his family left, they would have to take a long, circuitous route west and southeast,

---

[3]Pronounced Loo-tong-ah

to the nearest airport at Tshikapa,[4] where they might find seats on a commercial flight.

The national government had not taken kindly to the plans of Chief Kalonji to establish an autonomous tribal kingdom in South Kasai. National army troops were compelled to fight periodic savage battles to crush his rebellion; these same army troops manned roadblocks along key transportation arteries throughout the country. They could be vengeful toward a lone, fleeing Baluba refugee.

Self-appointed vigilante groups were known to ambush and assassinate dignitaries of tribes they felt threatened them; it had already happened to two political leaders disembarking from a plane at Tshikapa airport. Kazadi's heart cried out to God to know what to do.

What would he find in South Kasai if and when he got there? The ravages of hunger and civil war, yes. Beyond that, Gizenga, pro-Communist heir to the slain Lumumba, had established his headquarters at the northern city of Stanleyville. He had proclaimed himself ruler of Congo, and his troops were advancing toward South Kasai.

But what would be the consequences of Kazadi's remaining at Charlesville? His adamant refusal to leave would only feed rumors that he was waiting for a propitious moment to lead his tribesmen in ransacking the missionaries' houses and taking flight. Spies had brought him the news that Bakuba warriors were gathering weapons for an attack; warriors of his own tribe were mobilizing to repulse it. Tensions could only heighten. When violence erupted, it would mean war, bloodshed, death, and anarchy. He could not bear the thought of carrying these people's blood on his hands. He went into the house and spoke to his wife. "Bambamona, pack some suitcases. We're leaving."

By late afternoon chiefs had arrived and seated themselves on chairs under palm trees in the yard. Each was flanked by his armed supporters. While they parleyed with Kazadi, two truckloads of blue-helmeted United Nations troops arrived. It was their job to patrol the villages and to keep people at peace. A commanding officer disembarked and came toward where they were seated.

"Hello," he greeted. "How are things here?"

Kazadi stood. "All of us sitting here are friends who have lived here for years, he replied. "We are talking over our problems and settling them peacefully."

[4]Pronounced Chee-kah-pah

He learned that the convoy was headed for Tshikapa. He asked the commanding officer to take along his wife and son, and gave instructions where they were to be left. He helped Bambamona onto the high truck bed. Their son climbed over its side.

"Strengthen your heart, Mother," the pastor said. "We'll see each other again."

The convoy left. Under armed escort it would travel directly south and arrive at Tshikapa before him.

Kazadi returned to the chiefs and seated himself. He announced to them his plans to leave and explained his reasons. He gave the ring of mission keys to the chief spokesman of the predominant local Bakuba tribe and asked him and his people to take responsibility now for guarding the missionaries' things. He led in prayer, asking God to allow no one to do another ill, then shook hands in farewell. They dispersed quietly. He would take a Chevrolet carryall left by the missionaries. He sent a messenger to call a Catholic friend who could drive. Then he went into the house and stretched himself out on a wicker-seated armchair to relax and wait.

It was evening. Dusk was closing in. The house was empty. His body, wracked with fatigue, now hurt with the pangs of loneliness. An enveloping cloud of foreboding depressed him to the point of despair. Later he described the situation.

"I put my knees onto the floor by that chair and prayed. Because within myself I was suffering much, I prayed to God with stern words and with water in my eyes. I said, 'Father, we read in Your Word that the journeys of all people are in Your hands; any path originating from You must have a good ending. Does the path I am taking tonight start with You? In the way I'm planning to go, will it be good or bad? You see my trouble. Why don't You show me?'

"I sat myself onto the chair, fell asleep, and dreamed. I saw a great crowd of rejoicing women with whitewash marks on their bodies and leaves tied by vines around their waists. This is how they always used to celebrate the birth of a child or the arrival of a renowned guest. Some with hoes were busy cutting the path. Others, following them with brooms, were sweeping it clean. Others were sprinkling the new path with whitewash, preparing it for the honored guest to pass. Then a voice spoke clearly: 'Kazadi, go.' I awoke and rejoiced. I said, 'God my

Father is clearing and preparing a path ahead of me. I'll go. Things will be all right.' "

The chauffeur arrived. They loaded a fifty-gallon drum of gasoline into the carryall, along with the pastor's suitcase, and left. They traveled west through the country of the Bampende, a friendly tribe, and arrived at the mission station of Nyanga before dawn. From a mission treasurer there, Kazadi procured a loan of funds, signing over his coffee-hulling machine left at Charlesville as security. He drove to Tshikapa and was reunited with his family. United Nations troops and a friendly local government authority both informed him that the Congo army troops were hostile toward prominent Baluba; if they discovered him, they would not allow him to go to South Kasai. Military security checks at the airport made it impossible for him to escape by air from here. To delay longer would mean possible arrest and imprisonment. He loaded his family into the carryall. They left for the next nearest airport, at Kikwit, 275 miles away. If they reached it, perhaps more favorable circumstances there would allow them to escape.

They threaded their way along poorly maintained dirt roads in a northwesterly direction through the land of the Bampende. By late afternoon they were hungry, so they stopped at an isolated Portuguese palm oil factory. A black Christian worker appeared and recognized Kazadi. He sent a note to his wife in a nearby village to prepare food for them. They ate and then continued their flight through the hours of the night. Eventually the road narrowed to barely distinguishable tracks between tall walls of elephant grass; then it ended abruptly on the bank of a stream. Leaving their headlights turned on, they got out and looked. A decrepit wooden platform mounted onto rotting dugout canoes was deeply silted into the sand. The time was 4:00 A.M. There was nothing to do but wait.

Shortly after daybreak two men carrying drinking gourds appeared on the opposite shore; they had come to the palm trees along the stream to collect wine. They paused, startled. One of them called, ''What are you doing here?''

''We want to cross the river.''

''You can't cross here. They stopped crossing machines here long ago. You'll have to go back to the last fork in the road, and turn left. That will take you to the place where they cross machines downstream.''

"About how far is it to the ferry going back that way?"

"We don't know; maybe 130 kilometers."[5]

Kazadi stood pondering their problem. Finally his wife spoke.

"Well, what is your thinking?"

"Look, let's first pray to God. Let's have faith that God will put us across this stream."

"Why are you talking like that?" the chauffeur asked peevishly. "Don't you see how rotten those boards are? There's no way to cross here. Let's turn the car around and go."

"Do you know how much gas we'll use going that long distance? Where will we get more? Don't you know people may be following us who want to kill us? I have no desire to go anywhere. We want to pray now. You believe with me that God is going to put us across.

"Our Father in heaven," he said, "our bodies are tattered; our hearts are split; our strength is finished. You are a God of love. Are You going to allow us, Your children, to die on this riverbank in this land of strangers, pointlessly? No father of love would do that. Long ago You divided the Red Sea to allow the children of Israel to escape their pursurers. We abandon ourselves into Your hands. Make a way for us to get across this river. Amen."

They waited. Inner tensions began mounting.

"Isn't there anything to eat?" their son asked.

Bambamona dug into a basket and distributed ears of roasted corn left over from the day before. They munched the cobs clean and discarded them.

Kazadi's watch showed 10:00 A.M. In his heart he kept reminding God and himself of the dream.

"Do you still have your mind in that path of thinking that we're going to get across here?" his wife asked incredulously.

"Explain to all of us just how it is going to happen," added the chauffeur.

"My understanding is this: let's pray to God that He send people with hearts to help us. They'll put us across."

They both laughed at him.

"I'm telling you that I'm not turning this machine around and going somewhere else. I'm waiting here until God sends someone to help us. Why do we read in the Bible that when Elijah prayed, fire fell

[5] Eighty miles

from heaven and consumed the sacrifice? Why do we read that God helped the poor widow to escape her adversaries by filling her jars with oil? Now why is it impossible for God to put us across this river? We're staying here."

By eleven o'clock they were hungry. The dry-season sun burned hot. Tiny, black sweat bees tormented them. They had a growing fear of pursuers. Their infuriation and torment had broken down all communicatons. Each person sat alone, looking into a separate direction.

At noon a young man appeared on the other side of the river, put his bicycle into a small dugout, and crossed the stream. Touching shore near the car, he glanced up and cried with surprise.

"Ki-i-i-ya! Is that Father Matthew Kazadi?"

"Yes, it's me. Who are you?"

"Years ago you taught me in class at Charlesville. I was born at your Mukedi station. I work near Kikwit."

"Friend, I am overjoyed to see you. I have a hard problem here, which only you can do something about. If you cannot help us, we may die here."

"What kind of help do you need?"

"We want to cross this river."

"At this place?"

"Yes, right here."

The young man paused to ponder the situation. Then he said, "Well, if that is the problem, I see only one way to help you. I'll go to the village and call for men to come with shovels. They can clear away the sand and push the ferry across with the machine on it. What do you think?

"I beg of you to do it. Go call them."

The man mounted his bike; his legs drove the pedals furiously.

Bambamona questioned the stranger's integrity. "Did you notice how your words were like empty air to him?" she asked. "He carried them like dry straw."

"That village he mentioned, do you think it is nearby?" rejoined the chauffeur. "That young fellow has gone forever."

"No, he'll come back," Kazadi said.

In about an hour there was an approaching hubbub of chanting, singing, and whistle-blowing. About twenty men came with digging tools. After warm greetings, they went into the water and began to work.

Kazadi started removing his shoes to join them.

"No-o-o-o," they protested. "Haven't we come to help you? Sit down on that log over there. Rest yourself."

They dug the boats clear. They cut down two heavy saplings and paralleled them on the underside of a rotting approach-plank. The car crawled onto the platform. They loaded the two approach-planks. Lustily they sang a rhythmic chant, heaved in unison to break the boats free from the sand, pushed the ferry across the stream, repositioned the planks, and disembarked the vehicle. Inwardly Kazadi was shouting for joy. *Look how God is hoeing the path ahead of us,* he marveled.

Their job finished, the men stood waiting.

"What kind of pay do you ask for?"

"We want you to give us six hundred francs."[6]

He weighed their demand against his resources.

"Beloved brothers, for over forty years I've been a part of your country here. Some of you who put me across the river were born, my being present. For all these years I've taught you. I've taught your children. I never took a thing that belonged to you. All my work was to help you. Now in my old age, I'm finally returning to my home country. You should do more than put me across this river. You should give me a gift of money for us to buy food with along the way. Here you are saying, 'We want you to pay us.' Why can you not just say to one another, 'Our father who helped us all these years is finally on his journey homeward,' thank me, and wish me well on my way?"

Their response was spontaneous. They shouted, clapped, blew their whistles, and danced with joy. He drew three hundred francs from his billfold.

"Here is a thank-you gift for the good hearts you've shown us. Now let's all bow our heads and pray that God will help us in these hard days."

He prayed.

The men turned and left, chattering happily.

The journey continued. By nightfall they reached a friendly village on the western edge of the AIMM field. They stopped, ate, were shown to a hut, and retired. After midnight they were awakened by an excited ruckus at their door. *Our pursuers have overtaken us,* thought Kazadi, his body tensing again. He got up, cautiously opened the door, and was

[6]About $10.00

astounded to see Bampende students he had left in school at Charlesville.

"Ki-i-i-ya! My friends, what brings you here?" he asked.

"Oh, pastor, your leaving really stirred up things. That very night, village people from tribes on both sides of the river, some from far away, came and broke into the mission buildings. They ransacked them. They looted the missionaries' home. They ruined everything. The turmoil caught everybody. There was no one left to help us; so we all left. We didn't expect to find you here." The pastor talked to them reassuringly until they calmly dispersed.

At dawn Kazadi and his party arose, ate, and continued their journey. More and more, the road showed signs of heavier traffic; apparently they were approaching a city. Suddenly, they were confronted with a heavy pole slung across the road, supported on each end by a forked post. Seated to one side under a palm tree were four national army soldiers, guns in hand. It was a roadblock. The thought shot through Kazadi's mind, "Have these troops been alerted by the Tshikapa forces to arrest me? My God, the way You've already helped us, will You let me be caught here?" Soldiers ordered him out of the car; they escorted him to their officer seated behind a rickety table in a nearby hut.

"We need to inspect your things," he said.

"I don't have any things; all I have is a small suitcase in the car. Everything remained where I came from."

They brought his suitcase from the car and opened it. With his clothing they found a well-worn Bible, a hymnal, and medals awarded him by the Belgians for faithful service to the colony. They studied these items, replaced them, and closed the suitcase.

"You appear to be a person who is not mixed up in politics," the officer said. "So we have no reason to trouble you. But you are in our hands now. If we release you and you get killed in the road, we will carry responsibility for your death. I want to put you into the hands of two armed soldiers; they will go with you to Kikwit, show you the way to the home of a missionary couple, leave you in their hands, and then return."

"Thank you, sir. You have done us well."

They were escorted into the city to a missionary's residence. Two days later Kazadi and his family flew on a plane packed with refugees to Bakwanga, the capital city of the Baluba country of South Kasai. It was

July 7. At the airport they stood as disoriented strangers in the milling crowd. Then the pastor recognized a familiar face, that of a young man who had been a government authority at Tshikapa. He caught the man's attention and approached him.

"You have arrived here ahead of me?"

"What other place on earth remains for us to go to?" the man asked.

"Can you tell me where I might find some missionaries?"

"Of the missionaries here, the one you need to see is Lutonga."

On hearing the name, the pastor was stupefied.

"Our Lutonga? From Charlesville? Do you know where he sits?"

"Come. I'll drive you there in my car."

They reached the city. The air was polluted with dust, smoke, and obnoxious odors. They entered the short driveway of a cream-colored stucco dwelling behind a shrub fence and stopped. There was much activity in the backyard. Kazadi saw the tall, erect white-haired figure of his old friend approaching. The two men stared at each other; then they embraced and wept unashamedly. Lutonga, with a hand on the old man's shoulder, spoke.

"Pastor, this is your tribal fatherland. This is the town of your origin. But it was not good for you to come now. Affairs here are very hard."

"No. It's good for me to arrive at this time. How can I stay somewhere else among strangers? I want to be among my own tribal people. If they are dying, it's good that we die together."

It was near noon. Graber shared his meal with them. Then he proceeded to make arrangements for them.

"Now that you are here, what would you like to do?"

"Help me find some leaders of the church; to begin, we can sit with them."

Lutonga sent word. A pastor named Tshidibi and his friend came. Tshidibi was also a refugee; his face was puffed; an eye was badly swollen; the black pigment of exposed parts of his body was broken in numerous places with fresh red contusions. "Soldiers beat him and threw him into prison, only because of this independence business," the friend confided.

The two loaded Kazadi, his wife, and his son into a vehicle and drove to a point on the outskirts of town. They got out, picked up the baggage, and began to walk to the hut Tshidibi called "home," where he had put his belongings. The scene that met the newcomers' eyes left them numb with shock. It was the aftermath of war.

The rubble of destroyed homes was still smoldering. The air hung heavy with dust and smoke and the putrid odor of decaying flesh. They weaved their way through silent clusters of emaciated, hollow-eyed people sitting on the ground with their dead, gazing vacantly into space, shock overwhelming any sense of grief. An occasional abandoned corpse was too mutilated or decayed or dirty even to show distinction of sex. Then, involuntarily, the pastor's eyes were riveted onto a woman's corpse, bloated balloon-tight, her arms grotesquely stretched before her as if to fend off an invisible assailant.

Tshidibi led them to a makeshift shack of pieces of rusty sheet iron nailed onto sticks. They thanked him. Kazadi sat on a box and closed his eyes to interrupt the images. Never in all his years had he seen earth so devastated, people so wasted. The brutality, the suffering, the destruction, surged over him like a dark, suffocating wave.

He recalled that happy bygone era when tribes worshiped together; parents tilled their gardens and fields; children recited their lessons in thatch-roofed classrooms; families ate their food and slept unmolested under their hut roofs. That way of life was now shattered — pitilessly shattered by hate, division, famine, and war; it lingered only as a receding memory. How could such suffering be stopped? What would it take to put back together all this brokenness and bring back to him and his people that happy way of life again?

Kazadi knew that he had shared a meaningful pilgrimage with Lutonga for most of the years of their lives. He did not know that the most significant chapters of that relationship were yet to be written, and that from this association would eventually emerge answers to his questions. The story of that relationship begins when they first met in 1930.

2

... In the Beginning ...

IT WAS JUNE 25, 1930. Young Archie Graber awoke at daybreak and looked over at his wife, who was still sleeping The excitement of his new surroundings rapidly cleared his thinking. The air was refreshingly cool. Their mosquito net was damp with dry-season fog, which had filtered through a screened window. He looked through the net and let his eyes scan the room: the bamboo rattan ceiling to catch droppings from the thatch roof, the white-washed mud walls, the hard dirt floor partially covered with woven reed throwmats, the simple washstand with an enamel basin and a galvanized water bucket. He listened to tropical birds in the nearby jungle greet the morning with their brilliant, strange-sounding songs. His excitement heightened. This would be their first full day at Charlesville, Congo, the mission station that was to be their home.

Archie quietly slipped from bed, dressed, unlocked the front screen door, stepped out onto the small veranda, and settled himself comfortably into a creaking wicker chair. His eyes began to examine the compound, its details barely discernible through the fog. He was facing west. To his left, across a gently sloping, bare yard, was the rear of a missionary residence; it was one of four brick structures with painted metal roofs built along a neatly cleaned T-shaped path laced with planted palms. The T-intersection was behind him, its leg extended before him, running the full length of the compound. The scattered brick buildings stood like brave, tawny-brown, red-capped sentinels inconsonant with the surrounding primitive dusky green.

Across the path at a distance to his left, a large grassy expanse sloped slowly down to a wall of jungle, where the terrain graduated into steeper descent south toward the river. Ahead of him was a mishmash of stubborn patches of jungle undergrowth, thatch-roofed huts, and garden plots, reaching to the far end of the compound. There the T-leg path intersected with the well-worn public foot road which led down to the Kasai River, half a mile away, where their long journey had ended yesterday.

In a sense, yesterday's arrival was the culmination of two tumultuous months. Memories still fresh flooded his mind: graduation from Bible Institute, marriage, ordination, a four-week ocean voyage via Europe, a seven-day trip by river steamer through pristine inland forest, and finally, an unnerving two-day road trip in a touring car driven by a black-skinned Jehu. The trip brought them from that distant river port to the opposite bank of the Kasai River at the foot of the hill.

Senior missionaries and a hundred jubilant blacks were waiting to greet them. Graber, his wife, and their baggage were crossed to the north bank in dugout canoes. There they were seated in sedan chairs supported by bamboo poles, which were hoisted onto the shoulders of carriers. Then, to the lusty singing of the welcoming party, they were jostled rhythmically through the forest up the hill to the mission compound. Obviously, Graber mused, the work of his missionary predecessors was admirable; it was bearing fruit. How good God had been to put the jumbled pieces of his life together and to call him to share in such a work!

An Ohio farm boy, he had finished eight years in a one-room schoolhouse and then spurned further study. He drifted from job to job; he had been a carpenter, a metal worker at Fisher Body, a deck hand on a Great Lakes ore steamer, a western ranch hand, a millwright man. At age 24, he drove a spinster university teacher to her post on the West Coast. She persuaded him to enter high school. He completed it, with special study in art. Involvement with a group of Christian service students there initiated a three-year spiritual battle over the matter of full consecration. He finally surrendered to the call for full-time service at a Bible conference at Winona Lake, Indiana. A week later he enrolled at Moody Bible Institute, where he worked his way through in the carpenter shop, met his wife, received his call to Africa, and graduated.

Graber's thoughts were interrupted by a black boy wearing khaki shorts and a white kitchen apron, who brought him a note. He nodded his thanks, read it, and called into the house.

"Evelyn, they want us to come for breakfast."

She rose, dressed, and came out to join him. He took her hand as they stepped off the veranda. He was tall and slim with a slender, angular face, brown eyes, and straight brown hair neatly parted on the left; she was slender and stood just taller than his shoulders; neatly coiffured, wavy black hair parted in the middle accentuated her delicately formed face. They walked to the residence of a woman missionary, where they were warmly welcomed, and enjoyed a breakfast of papaya, sweet rolls, oatmeal, and coffee. They finished eating and went to sit in the living room. Then the senior missionary, responsible for overseeing station activities, arrived to take them on a tour of the station.

"Before we leave," he said, "I should give you some background information. In the old days a river port was established here because Wissman Falls makes this the end point for water navigation. The Company of Kasai first used the port for exporting rubber latex they gathered here. Later the Belgians opened a diamond-mining operation, and the Belgian colonial government established an outpost for civil administration. People from various tribes came seeking employment with these enterprises and settled here. So it has become a large center of population."

"About how many different tribes live here?" Graber asked.

"At least half a dozen. Tribal names are difficult for newcomers to remember. For now you should be aware of three. The Bakuba tribespeople are native to this side of the river. When missionaries first arrived eighteen years ago, the Bakuba chief, Djoko Punda, gave them this plot of ground on which to build a station. At that time he and other area chiefs covenanted that this plot of ground would be hallowed; it was made off-limits to any killing and malevolent deeds by witchcraft."

He continued speaking without interruption, over the clatter of dishes the black boy was clearing off the table.

"Across the river is territory of the Lulua tribe. In history they were a fierce warring people. They secured guns from Portuguese traders and collaborated with them in slave traffic. The Baluba tribespeople border the Lulua several hundred miles east of here. Originally the two tribes were of blood kinship; but the Lulua, with their imported guns, subdued the Baluba and kept some of them as slaves. The Baluba are a more quiet, industrious people and are quite independent of spirit. They recognized more quickly than others that the future lies with those who get an education and settle into well-paying jobs. This they can do now, because Belgians rule the colony with an iron hand.''

"Are the Baluba more ready to respond to the gospel?'' Graber asked.

"In general, I would say so. They may also see the mission as offering them an outlet for their suppressed ambitions. The majority of our leaders come from the Baluba tribe. But the mission is attracting people from a variety of tribes. They see it as something of a haven. Often when families in the outlying areas are converted, they want to separate themselves from pagan practices in the villages. So they come to settle here. The mission provides education for their children. It has medicine when they get sick. There is land nearby where they can make fields and raise their food. Here we hope people from different tribes will begin to learn what it means to be one people in Christ. They live in what we call 'the Christian village' just off the north edge of the mission compound. For the most part, Bakuba people have continued to live in their traditional villages; they've been slower to take to the ways of the white man. Predominant tribal groups in the Christian village here are Lulua and Baluba. They build their huts in their respective tribal sections of the village, but in church you can seldom tell them apart. Don't hesitate to ask questions. Now let's go for a walk.''

He stood up and walked out ahead of them. Archie and Evelyn were not sure there was time for questions. It seemed their senior colleague was as somber and resolute as a river rushing down its channel, and they were about to be caught in the current. Evelyn hastily thanked their hostess. Archie held the screen door open for her. In passing, she looked up at him; it was at such times that his mischievous smile and twinkling eyes suggested that the two of them were sharing a childhood adventure together.

They followed the long path Graber had seen earlier that morning. It led them east to the T-intersection, and then directly to the front of the church, a long, low, rectangular brick building with a red corrugated iron roof. It had a tall, square bell tower centered in the front wall, with an entry door on either side. They entered. Graber, interested in architecture, noticed the darkish interior, the substantial size, the dirt floor, the backless board seats, and several interior brick columns supporting rafters.

"Is it full on the Lord's Day?" Graber asked.

"No. Its size is ample. But on special days like Christmas, it is packed."

From the church they walked south, in the direction of the river, down a slight grade for thirty yards, to the house the Grabers were to occupy. It was an L-shaped brick structure, the base of the L forming the living quarters and facing west. It was fronted by a narrow-roofed veranda, with cement steps midway along its length. On either side of the steps was a row of square, brick, roof-support columns, one of them graced with a climbing bougainvillea vine. Column bases were connected by two low, parallel rows of bricks, which formed a series of flower boxes. That part of the house forming the leg of the L pointed east, parallel with the church. In it a dining room opened onto a large, screened breezeway and to a kitchen on the far end.

Between the backyard of the house and the church, near the wall of encroaching jungle, sat a native hut. Near it was a corrallike enclosure of crooked, weather-beaten sticks.

"This is where Mbuyi, the goatherd, lives. We have about twenty goats which furnish us milk. Unfortunately, there are never enough missionary hands to do everything. We want you to take responsibility for Mbuyi and his work. This means seeing that he milks the goats every morning and brings milk to our houses to boil in time for breakfast. Now let's go into the forest to where they are making bricks."

They entered a forest path that led them down the hill toward the river. Sometimes it took the form of a tunnel, bored through the heavy, interwoven mesh of vines, thorny undergrowth, and sprawling limbs. Again the growth would recede from their sides, forming what seemed like a great, walled cathedral of nature, ceiled with blackish lace of shifting leaves against the clearing azure sky. The air was heavy, moist, rich with the odor of plant humus, which formed a thick-piled carpet on the forest floor. Once the sound of their walking was interrupted by the crashing of leafy branches to one side of them; a bevy of foraging monkeys had taken flight. Suddenly the path broke into a sun-bathed clearing near the river's edge. Pressed, gray clay bricks were stacked in a pile shaped like a huge pup tent, twenty feet long and fifteen feet high.

Men were busy making bricks with two primitive hand presses, each operated by raising and lowering a heavy wooden pole.

"The home office probably told you we've needed someone to help us with building construction. We have plans for a building that will provide space for offices, a printing press, and storing supplies. There are seventy thousand bricks stacked in this kiln. Your first big job is to bake them. It takes six days of firing to do the job right: three days of slow heat and three days of intense heat. After that, you'll be ready to start construction. We have a good team of men in the carpenter shop to help you with woodwork. Now you should meet our native church leaders."

On leaving, Archie returned a glance from Evelyn with a look of quiet desperation. He was to begin work already? What was the word for "goat" . . . or for "brick"? Were such work assignments to be accomplished by means of sign language? They trudged back up the hill, across the station compound to a hut on the edge of the Christian village. In the backyard a black man, apparently a bit older than Graber, sat on a straight-backed chair. As they approached, he smiled, rose, and warmly shook hands with each of them. He was of medium height, sturdy build, and seemingly quiet demeanor. The senior missionary exchanged some unintelligible words with the man; then he turned to Graber and his wife.

"This man's name is Luaba.[1] He is one of our first baptized Christians. He's from the Baluba tribe. As a child he worked as table boy for Mr. and Mrs. Haigh, the first missionaries here. Luaba is the leader of our native church work. He spends a lot of time traveling on foot to visit Christians in villages throughout our region, and to encourage village boys and girls to come to live here to study. He is our first candidate to be ordained as an assistant pastor. You will be in charge of our evangelistic work in the villages, so you'll probably be traveling a lot with him. Now let's go to the Bible school."

Graber's mounting frustration pressed him toward dismay. He and Evelyn nodded farewell to the black man and followed their colleague.

"While the Baluba are a more quiet, industrious people," the senior missionary continued, "this does not mean that they do not differ in personality. Luaba, the man you just met, has been with us since a child. He has caught onto our ways. He is easy to get along with. But the

[1]Pronounced Lwah-bah

Archie and Evelyn Graber

Matthew Kazadi

leader I'm going to introduce you to now was first a student in Catholic schools. He's had a sound conversion experience; he is a gifted teacher and has real possibilities. But he is a bit more independent. He has a mind of his own and isn't always so ready to carry out instructions.''

A tall, gangling black man about Graber's age stood before a line of students outside a row of thatch-roofed, one-room, shedlike structures which served as classrooms. His quiet, firm voice, punctuated with a prodding forefinger, held their attention. He was giving them some kind of instructions. The missionaries approached him.

"This man's name is Matthew Kazadi."

They shook hands.

"Kazadi is responsible for boy students who come in from the villages and live here. There are about ninety. He teaches them in the classroom. He also sees that they make fields here for food, in order to be self-supporting. They live in their own huts to one side of the compound, so he can supervise them outside of class hours. When some of them are converted, learn to read, and know something of the Bible, we send them into the villages for two weeks to do evangelistic work. Kazadi has finished teaching this class; they're about to leave for the villages. Evelyn, you are a musician. These schoolchildren sing well. Maybe you can train some of them."

Years later Kazadi described the moment. "While we stood there that day, the old missionary said to me, 'This young man who has just come is a hard worker in two ways: in preaching and in working with his hands. Kazadi, I want you to be a strong helper to him. Stand by his side; always strengthen his arms in the work.' In those days, to us black people the white man was big chief. As was the custom of that time, we respected and feared and obeyed him. To whatever he said, our answer was one: 'Yes, sir. So be it.' We had become accustomed to the role of the white man, whether he was a government authority or a missionary. But we had hope for something fresh and new. As was the custom, we black leaders chose African names for new missionaries. This new man's name, we decided, would be 'Lutonga,' which means 'sprout' . . . something fresh and green growing out of a dry stump; and his wife's name would be 'Mutekemena,' which means 'hope.' ''

3

... Fragile Roots ...

EVELYN HELPED THE table boy put away the breakfast dishes. Then she gathered her study materials and sat down at the dining-room table to prepare for her language lesson. She made a few faltering efforts to begin and then decided it was impossible. Her mind was drawn to a more immediate concern. In fact, she was worried.

Since that first day, Archie's frustrations had not subsided. He had been allowed no time for language study. He was immediately assigned multiple duties, which he felt at loss to discharge responsibly. He feared the repercussions if he should inadvertently make a mistake. She hurt for Archie. She understood his situation. It held the explosive ingredients of conflict for black and white. That's what made her anxious. She hoped and prayed that he would find his way through these early months without an incident that might provoke irresolvable misunderstanding.

But since what happened at breakfast that morning, she wondered. They had almost finished eating when a messenger came with a note: Archie and Mbuyi, the goatherd, were to come to the senior missionary's house. What could this mean? Inasmuch as she couldn't study, she might just as well sit and wait.

Her thoughts were drawn to Mbuyi. At first she had considered him a rather peculiar-looking fellow, with his pudgy, pock-marked face, his short wiry frame, and his knobby knees. She wondered how his wife, Delela, had been attracted to him. But their hut sat just off the backyard, perhaps a hundred feet from her breezeway doorstep; so Archie and Evelyn had quickly become acquainted with them. As she came to understand their way of life, she recognized the strengthening bonds of a deep friendship. Moreover, in Mbuyi she sensed a gentleness, earnestness, and strength which were compelling.

Mbuyi was a typical tribesman of that time. During the week he wore threadbare khaki shorts or faded blue denim shorts with incongruous patches fraying at the seams. Sometimes he wore a T-shirt so tattered she wondered how he found his way into it. Everyone in the more progressive tribes strove to emulate the white man. That meant wearing a shirt, even if it exposed more skin than it covered.

On Sundays Mbuyi wore ready-made clothing, which had begun to appear in the local trading centers. He had purchased one pair of long white trousers and a long-sleeved white shirt, cast-off garments from some white man's wardrobe across the great water. They were always wrinkled; he owned no iron. He never wore shoes.

When herding the goats or when taking a foot-journey, his only weapon was a long-handled, hardwood cudgel, shiny from use, which also served as a walking staff. At work, his principal tool was a long-bladed, single-edged machete — heavy enough to hack brush when clearing land for his garden and sharp enough to pare a narrow dry strip of bamboo to a sharp, fine point to extract a jigger buried beneath a toenail.

Evelyn admired Delela and her tribal sisters for their skills. She marveled that they could find fulfillment in their arduous duties. She had watched Delela routinely carry a huge enamel basin of water from the spring and set it down at the hut doorstep without spilling a drop. She had seen her hoeing their garden for half an hour, straight-kneed, bowed sharply at the waist until her brow was hardly a foot from the ground. For African women, the close-fitting, one-piece, western-style dress was too constricting. A loose cloth tucked around the waist and draping to well below the knees allowed freedom of body movement, and a loose-bottomed short blouse allowed ready access to a breast to pacify or feed their small children.

The spiritual need of the Africans was obvious. Their fear of malevolent spirits was frightening; and the rites connected with their ancestral worship were often disgusting. But Evelyn and Archie had often remarked that they seemingly found contentment in the barest necessities of life. The mud-walled, thatch-roofed home of Mbuyi and Delela was no more than seven feet square. Their daily diet was simple:

a sticky mush made of manioc and corn flour shaped into a loaf and eaten with the fingers, a side dish of greens cooked in palm oil, and occasionally the luxury of fresh meat. At night, Mbuyi slept on a low, rectangular bamboo platform with a single blanket; Delela slept on a mat on the dirt floor by a burning fire. It provided warmth against the chill and smoke to discourage insect pests.

Evelyn was learning to love these people. How can you love people without hurting with them? Her heart wanted to respond to all the hurts around her, but there were those who warned that open-handed generosity would promote childlike dependency and beggarism. How and where was one to draw the line? Sometimes she allowed the hurts of others to affect her so deeply that she became depressed with their burden. Perhaps she did need to put a tighter rein on her emotions. Maybe she shouldn't allow herself to be too concerned about what happened this morning.

The breezeway screen door slammed shut, startling her. Archie stalked into the dining room and sat down at the table. His face showed exasperation.

"Evelyn, I'm ready to pack my suitcase and go home."

"What's happened?"

"Do you remember at the missionary meeting the other night when they complained about strong goat scent in the milk and said that ought not to be? Well, it all came out into the open this morning."

"What do you mean?"

"That's what the message was about. The missionaries began questioning Mbuyi. I couldn't understand their conversation with him, but apparently something was pretty bad. Afterwards they explained to me that Mbuyi has been neglecting to pen the kids away from their mothers at night. So when he milks the goats in the morning, he comes up short of milk."

"So?"

"Well, he didn't want to make anybody angry because he didn't have enough milk to go around. So he has been adding a little water from the udder-washing bucket."

"Oh, no!"

Archie paused, his frustration simmering.

"I was made to know that every night before bedtime I'm to see that those kids are separated from their mothers. And I'm to get Mbuyi up at daybreak every morning to see that he does his job on time. Honey, I've been working myself to death to meet people's expectations of me, and I'm still not measuring up. What's the use of staying here if we're just going to disappoint people?"

"Maybe we're too concerned about disappointing people. Maybe we just have to be ourselves. When we arrived, don't you remember how it seemed that missionaries were overscheduling themselves? Now you're driving yourself as hard as any of them."

"I have to, with all the work there is to do. I can cope with work. But why do we missionaries have to saddle ourselves with every detail? Before I went to spend those nights in the forest burning bricks, I showed Mbuyi what his job was, and I expected him to do it. How will the people of this country ever learn to do anything for themselves if we don't give them responsibility? And when one of them under our supervision makes a mistake, why are we made to feel it is the unpardonable sin?"

"Now, honey, maybe we don't understand all the stresses missionaries have to work under."

"But I can't be standing over people all the time. Can't the rules we work with allow for a little bit of human frailty? Why are missionaries so strong-willed?"

"Well, maybe you have to be strong-willed to survive on the mission field. And if that's what it takes, dear," a smile curled on her lips, "I think you'll make it. Don't we still believe that the Lord called us here? He answered prayer in so many wonderful ways to confirm it, I don't think that this one incident has changed His mind. He'll help us to be loving, even at times when we don't understand everything. Besides, I'm beginning to realize how much I really love these African people. And I think they care about us too."

Archie drummed his fingers on the table, contemplating. Maybe Evelyn was right. Occasional incidents were cropping up which seemed to show it. Take, for example, that time at the building construction site, when he roundly scolded a workman and thought he had done a good job. Later the foreman came to him privately and counseled him on how to improve on his method. What was that but a vote of confidence?

The memory of such incidents gave Archie some hope. He knew that Congolese were reluctant to openly express their feelings about a white man. This probably made such cues even more significant. What he didn't know was that they were outcrops of much stronger opinions which Congolese were sharing clandestinely.[1]

One morning Graber entered the carpenter shop, a long, rectangular, metal-roofed, brick building set just north of the guesthouse where he and Evelyn had stayed when they first arrived, and near where masons were busy erecting walls of the new building. He was under pressure. From a distant missionary establishing a new station he had received an order for panel doors to be installed in the buildings. He had begun making door and window frames for the new office-press building.

Graber was not totally unprepared for this work load at the carpenter shop. When he had been given supervision of the building program, he recognized that eight carpenters would not meet its demands. He hired eight new men interested in learning woodworking and assigned each of them to a carpenter as an apprentice. Hopefully this way he could handle a greater volume of work and, at the same time, teach new men a trade.

Hand-planing the rough-sawn lumber was the biggest job. It seemed to take an eternity to plane a board smooth. Now, at half a dozen workbenches men were busy planing; at two others they were mortising and assembling. As Graber moved from bench to bench, he felt disappointed at the men's slow progress. He searched his meager vocabulary for appropriate words to press them to their tasks.

"Hurry up, men," he cried out, "or we won't finish forever."

He took a plane from a carpenter, dismantled it, and checked its blade. It was dull. He had repeatedly demonstrated the importance of keeping their tools sharp to properly work the forest's stubborn cross-grained hardwoods. This man had forgotten. Graber got the honing stone, told the man and his helper to watch, honed the blade to a fine edge, replaced it, and planed a few strokes to demonstrate its improvement.

Then he proceeded to the next table, discovered the identical problem, and remedied it. He visited all six tables, repeating the routine. They had all forgotten. He scolded them each in turn for not taking his instructions seriously.

At an assembly bench an apprentice was struggling with a pinching

[1]Conversations in the following incident are structured to fit documented prevailing feelings of that time.

saw. Graber laid it flat on a board, asked the carpenter and helper to watch, placed the head of a large nail onto a tooth, and firmly struck the nail point with a hammer. In this manner he set alternate teeth the full length of the blade. He reversed the saw, setting the other side. He sharpened the teeth and returned the saw. The apprentice, upon discovering the saw's new cutting ability, gave himself to his work with renewed energy.

Graber proceeded to the next bench and began checking the men's tools. Chisels too were dull from overuse. His frustration was mounting. Apparently, up to the present, all his instruction about tool care had been fruitless. Then the carpenter from the previous bench came and touched his elbow.

"Come here," he said.

Graber returned with him to his bench. The apprentice, over-enthusiastic about his freshly sharpened saw, had missed the mark and cut off a planed door-frame board half an inch short.

Graber lost his temper.

"Why did you do that? A good board like that! Now its's useless. You did bad . . . very bad. Your work is worthless."

He struck the board with his hand for emphasis and stormed out of the building.

The apprentice, dismayed, looked at his supervisor.

"I've ruined my chance of learning," he said, shaking his head. "I've killed my friendship with that white chief forever. How will I ever look at him face to face again?"

"No, it is not like that," a nearby carpenter said. "Lutonga doesn't keep his anger for long. He's not driving you away. He wants to be everybody's friend. You made a mistake accidentally. That made him sad. He hasn't rejected you. Just try harder to do like he says."

"Lutonga can't say much yet," said another. "But his acts show us he counts us people of worth. Those nights when they burnt the bricks, he forsook his wife and took his camp cot out into the woods and slept with black people. He still being on his honeymoon! Amazing thing. Out there he shared his food with the workmen. He dirtied his hands with work like everybody else. Some protested, but he said, no, he was one of us."

"Our church leaders Luaba and Kazadi noticed the same thing the day Lutonga arrived," said another. "When he got out of the dugout he wanted to take a picture. He gave his camera bag to a boy to hold for him . . . a stranger, a child he'd never seen before. He wasn't afraid he might lose his thing. He trusts us.''

Graber reentered the building. They cut off their conversation. He went to the offending apprentice, put his hand on his shoulder, looked at him through eyes welling with tears, and said, "I did badly. Anger caught me. I am your friend. Take hold of your work. Do it right. Go forward.''

He perfunctorily adjusted a few tools on the bench and left.

The carpenter looked at his apprentice and nodded knowingly. The apprentice shook his head incredulously, sighed, and frowned in deep concentration as he studied the numbers on his measuring tape to mark a fresh board.

4

... How to Win a Girl Friend ...

ARCHIE AND EVELYN found it impossible to love the people without sharing their hurts. They also discovered that hurts could not be healed without some degree of personal cost to themselves.

One afternoon a week Graber joined eight black church council members in hearing disputes involving fellow Christians. They held their weekly session in the church, the council members sitting in a semicircle in front of the rostrum, with Graber at the left end and Kazadi next to him, on his right. Luaba, sitting midway, was chairman. The litigants sat in a queue on the grass outside the church and presented themselves before the council in turn.

Graber sat in his place late one afternoon, hoping the session would end soon. His mind was weary from his efforts to decipher the endless torrent of strange sounds. He felt he had sat there long enough to discharge his responsibility. Moreover, he needed to check the progress of his workmen before quitting time.

The last of those waiting entered the front door of the church and came down the center aisle . . . a man, his wife, and their daughter, perhaps twelve, tugging at her mother's hand, her face wet with weeping.

"These are Christians from a village in the hills," Luaba explained to Graber.

Following them came a tall old man wearing a misshapen felt hat and a full-length army surplus overcoat. As he approached the front of the church, light from the side entryways filled in the details. His hat was a dirty brownish-green; his furrowed face wore a bristle of gray whiskers; his soiled, buttonless coat hung open, revealing kinky gray chest hair and a wasted bony torso. His thighs were wrapped with a piece of grimy raffia cloth held in place by a vine tied around the waist.

The family took places on a front church bench to the left side; the old man sat down across the aisle from them.

"Who has a word?" Luaba asked.

The old man stood and took his position before the council.

"These people won't give me my wife," he said, motioning to the girl. "I wanted to go to the white government man to get justice, but her parents said we should come here first."

There was a pause. Graber was sure he understood the old man's words. He wrinkled his forehead in disbelief.

"When did you start paying the parents bride price for her?" asked Luaba.

"As is the custom in our tribe, a man covenants for a wife before she is born. When he sees a woman who is pregnant, he brings her the gift of a chicken and says, 'If your baby is a girl, she will be my wife; if it is a boy, he will be my special friend.' If the woman agrees, she accepts the chicken, they eat a meal, and the covenant is closed."

"What proof do you have that you closed such a covenant with the mother of this girl?"

"I will show you." The man dug a hand deep into an overcoat pocket and extracted a dry, discolored bone. "This is the leg-bone of the covenant chicken we ate together that day."

Graber watched tears course freely down the girl's sad face. The beauty, purity, and strength of this innocent child would be squandered by this old man? The thought of it was revolting. He wondered what plan the council would devise to free her.

"Have you finished paying the bride price the parents demand?" Luaba asked.

"Yes, I finished the debt: two goats and five hundred francs."

"Does anyone else have a question to ask him?"

Council members were silent. The old man returned to sit on the bench. Luaba motioned for the girl's father to come stand in the same place.

"Have you heard the words of this man?"

"Yes."

"You and your wife, did you agree for him to begin a marriage contract for your daughter?"

"Yes."

"Has he finished paying you the bride price you requested?"

"Yes."

Graber was appalled.

"But why?" he interjected. "Why did you agree to that?"

"White man, at that time we did not know Jesus. We simply followed the custom of our ancestors."

Kazadi murmured to Archie behind the flat of a hand, "Among us, the man who is a nonbeliever doesn't consider a girl child to be of great value. He only thinks about the bride price that somebody will pay for her when she is old enough to be married."

Council members briefly consulted together. Then one of them spoke to the father.

"There is only one way to dissolve such a marriage covenant. That is to reimburse the man the bride price he paid you."

"That wealth he gave us was spent long ago. Where could we find it now to reimburse him?"

"Don't you have any livestock?"

"No."

"What about your relatives? Can't they help you?"

"I have only one brother. He has nothing either."

The girl broke into uncontrollable sobs. The mother slipped an arm around her in a futile effort to comfort her.

Graber scrutinized the old man's leathery, deeply wrinkled face. He could detect no gentleness there, only crudeness, vulgarity, and even savagery. Compassion welled up in him. Then he thought of a way to save the girl.

"We have money," he said. "Money in the church box. Offerings people give on Sundays."

The council members were respectfully silent for a moment; then one spoke.

"That money is used to pay our church leaders and our village workers. If we used it to redeem this girl, how would they feel? They would not be happy."

"We must guard the church-box money for the purpose for which it has been given," said another. "If we start using it to untangle people from their problems, it will always be empty.''

They asked the litigants to wait outside, consulted each other briefly, and then recalled them. Luaba stood, looked at the couple, and spoke.

''You are Christians. But you must abide by the terms of your original covenant. If you want to show love for your daughter, you will reimburse the man his wealth. He will be satisfied, and she will be free. Does anyone have further words?''

All were silent.

''Then we have finished. Let us go to our places.''

Graber could hardly believe his ears. Would a church council actually throw a helpless young girl to an old wolf like this?

Council members stood and began filing out. The girl wailed, her body shaking with convulsive grief. Her mother scolded and pulled her to her feet. The sun had set. Archie rose and walked disconsolately across the yard toward his home. Surely Christians should be able to find an answer to such cruelty! He knew he would lie awake tonight wrestling with the problem.

''White chief! My chief!''

He stopped and turned. It was the girl. She caught his hand and gripped it in both of hers.

''Don't let me be married to that old man!'' she cried. ''Take me to be your child. I'll do anything you ask me to.''

Graber resumed walking toward home, the girl beside him, her tugging hands and pleas rending his heart. At the breezeway screen door he stopped, looked at her, and said, ''My child, I need to go into the house.'' She released her grip.

Archie went inside and recounted the incident to Evelyn, the sobbing girl still at the door.

''Is there a way we can help?'' his wife asked.

''We can take fifty-five dollars of our personal money, give it to the old man, and set the girl free. I know that is a lot of money the way things are now. But if I were in that girl's place, how would I feel? Or if we were parents and saw that happening to our daughter, what would we do?''

''If we pay her redemption price,'' Evelyn replied, ''this means we become her parents. Would she come to live in our home?''

''Why would that be necessary? We have dormitories here for girl students. Why can't she stay there and go to school with them?"

Graber strode out the door and called in the direction of the goatherd's hut.

"Mbuyi! Mbuyi! Go to the village. Call back the council members. Hurry."

To the girl he said, "Stop crying, my child. We are paying off your debt."

She was ecstatic. She leaped up and down, clapping her hands and squealing with delight.

Council members returned, and they concluded the matter. Graber did lie awake for awhile that night. He couldn't forget the girl's joy.

5

... Omen of Conflict ...

GRABER WAS NOT only in charge of building construction and maintenance at Charlesville, but he also was responsible for overseeing the work of evangelism in the station's assigned territory. This meant organizing his station duties so that he could schedule periodic trips with Luaba through outlying villages.

One mid-afternoon at the end of such a trip, Graber finished loading his camping equipment into the Model A, jumped into the driver's seat beside Luaba, slammed the door, and started the motor. He returned a final happy wave to bystanding villagers, pulled away from the hut where they had spent the night, twisted the steering wheel to turn the car onto the dirt road, and took off for home. He drove a car the way he drove himself . . . as if he always had to make up for lost time. He hoped to make it to Charlesville by dark.

As always, he had mixed feelings about returning. It would be good to see Evelyn. He needed to check workmen's progress with the building program. But living on a mission station, seeing the same faces, and coping with the same pattern of problems day after day was draining. His experience these past days had confirmed this fact again: his heart was in the villages. Here he sensed freedom and joy.

While he fastened his eyes on the narrow road ahead of him, his mind began replaying a sequence of happy scenes. He recalled night bonfires encircled by tight clusters of Christians singing hymns and giving testimonies. He remembered grass-roofed chapels with rows of attentive people sitting packed tight on makeshift benches of split logs.

There was that termite-ridden shelter in which they prayed for a sick widow, frail in body but radiant in her faith. Then he remembered the night he was kept awake by rats gnawing and rattling ear corn stored on top of the hut ceiling above him. He recalled smoky kitchen shacks emitting the aroma of chicken frying in palm oil.

People in the villages were warm, generous, appreciative, he reflected. A chief gave him a goat; it was butchered, cooked, and shared on the spot. A teacher vacated his hut, including a hen with "biddies," to make room for his cot. Children delivered water gourds fresh-filled from the forest spring. Women brought gifts of firewood, chickens, pineapples, papaya. Men cut down palm fronds and constructed him an outhouse. What was all this but their way of saying, "We love you!" He was preaching simple sermons now; he illustrated them with colored chalk sketches; and when he gave invitations, people came to Christ! What a pity he didn't know the language better. He had tried to study when there was time, but he found it hard. Nevertheless, when people learned that he really cared for them, it seemed they didn't notice his language mistakes. His heart rejoiced.

In the road ahead of him a scrawny hog lay soaking in a wallow. He honked the klaxon and cut his speed. The hog reluctantly rose, dripping mud, and sauntered into the grass.

Archie knew that the good will he found in the villages for the cause of the mission was largely the result of periodic visits Luaba had made on foot, during the years prior to his arrival on the field. Recently missionaries had honored Luaba's long faithfulness. They had ordained him to the highest church post then available to blacks: that of assistant pastor. Now Graber sought to encourage him in his work.

"I am happy to work in the villages," he ventured to Luaba.

"Say that again," the black man called over the noise of the motor.

Graber raised his voice. "I like to work in the villages. That work gives me much joy."

The man nodded in assent.

"People have good hearts. They know us. They love us. Because for many years you came to visit them. You have done good work."

The man was at a loss to know how to respond to the compliment.

The car approached a sand pit. Archie jammed the gear-shift rod into second, gave it the gas, and tensed on the wheel while the tires ground their way through, then reshifted into high.

"On this journey we baptized many people," he continued. "Yesterday seventy-five. All of these people, why are they coming to Jesus? Because you sowed the seed. You have worked hard. Now you see the fruit."

Yesterday's baptismal scene was still fresh in his mind: the long line of quiet, reverent candidates extending from river's edge up the hill; he and Luaba standing in waist-deep water sharing baptismal duties; then, in garments still dripping, the trip back to the village, all singing boisterously, "There is power . . . power . . . power in the blood . . . ," a long single file up the hill, moving slowly, deliberately, lest their joy end too soon. Graber never failed to thrill at such a scene.

"In days past, white men baptized. White men gave Communion. You were their helper. People looked up to them. But now you are their pastor. You baptize. You give Communion. These people are your sheep. You are their shepherd. You understand, do you not?"

The black man nodded gravely.

"A shepherd knows all his sheep," Archie continued. "He does not forget one of them. When we arrive at a village, we shake hands with everybody. We go to the chief's house and sit with him. We go to the homes of those who are sick to pray for them. We listen to the problems of the village mission teacher and his wife. We do thus to show people that we know all of them. We count them as precious."

Graber jerked the steering wheel to dodge a scampering goat. He recalled a problem encountered a few days earler. Tshibuele and her husband had both grown up on the mission station and attended its school. At that time she was a fine Christian. After marriage they went to an outlying village as mission teachers. When Graber visited the village now, Tshibuele called him to her hut. She explained that her husband had become dissatisfied, had quit teaching, and had taken a second wife. She wept, saying that now her life was in ruins.

"We can't resolve everybody's problems," he went on. "Like the problem of Tshibuele. But we can always pray with them. Thus they see that we have hearts to help them. They see that we care about them."

The black man was pondering. Gradually his brow furrowed. At length he spoke.

"White chief, I have a question."

"Speak."

"We have been in the path for two weeks. Because we traveled in this machine, we visited a good number of villages. But they were only a few. In my territory there are hundreds of villages. Christians in those villages exceed a thousand. You have the work of construction. You stay on the station much of the time. I journey on foot. You are telling me to do the work of a shepherd. But how can I shepherd this many sheep?"

"Truly, the villages are many," Graber replied. "You are one person. You can't do everything. I said these people are your sheep. I did not say it right. They are God's sheep. God is giving us these people. Because God is giving them to us, we must arrange a way to take care of them. This work is too great for one person. In the days ahead we will choose other mature men to become pastors. They will help you carry this burden."

Luaba's face was a mask. Archie wondered if his companion had understood his words.

"Did I answer your question?"

"I heard."

They entered the deep shadows of a heavy forest. Its moist, cool air tempered the hot motor odors filtering through the floorboard. Luaba seemed no longer disposed to conversation. Graber wondered if he had said something wrong. They traveled in silence the rest of the way home.

Over the following days Pastor Luaba struggled with the implications of Graber's words. From the day the missionaries had first arrived to the present, no one had served as faithfully as he. They gave him responsibility for the church; he carried it alone and well. He was chairman of church council on the station. He traveled to the four corners of the territory; when he returned, he brought people in the church news from worlds they had never seen. They held him in extraordinary esteem. Now missionaries talked of ordaining additional men as pastors. Why must he share with less-experienced, less-worthy men the prestige of his hard-earned position?

He shared his apprehension with a few close friends.

"You surpass all others in maturity and experience; no one doubts that," counseled some. "But you have the wisdom of one person. The church is not of one person. It is of God. If it is to grow and to reach people of all tribes, it needs the wisdom of several leaders. The hunter's net is made of many strands. A group of leaders will have wisdom to scold and encourage every person in a way he understands. Lutonga has spoken well."

Others gave him different advice. "Missionaries may think it is good wisdom to choose more leaders. But you know us black people," they warned. "When men younger than you see this door opened before them, they'll not be content to be your equal. They will want to wipe you out. You're a mature man . . . a wise man. Use your good sense. Take precautions. Do what needs to be done to frustrate their intentions. Don't let those youngsters find you with the wisdom of a little child."

6

... Angel of the Lord ...

GRABER REPEATEDLY witnessed the kindness of people in the villages. He was convinced of their sincerity. He did not entertain the thought that some among them might harbor malevolent intentions.

Ilolo was a village eighty miles west of Charlesville. One day it was the site of an important convocation. Half a dozen clan chiefs from area villages had gathered there. Now they sat on low stools in a circle in the shade of towering palms, just outside the circumference of huts. Each of them wore a long, full, raffia skirt and the appurtenances of chieftainship: heavy copper bracelets and anklets, a hat or bandolier with diagonal designs of bright-colored beads and cowry shells, decorative spherical tufts suspended along the fringe of a skirt. Village life went on around them, people maintaining a distance respecting the privacy of superiors in august deliberation.

Their tribe, in a prolonged war, continued to take heavy losses. Leaders and people together had exhausted traditional means of invoking the aid of their ancestral spirits. So they decided to call a distant witch doctor, renowned for making powerful medicines. Surely he could give them the key to break their enemies' magical power. He had arrived now. The assembled clan chiefs had explained their dilemma to him and paid his fee. He had taken a white chicken and had disappeared down a nearby high-grass footpath to talk with the spirits while the chiefs waited.

There was a rustle of grass. Heads jerked toward the path. The witch doctor emerged empty-handed. His head was covered with a skull cap bearing long black-and-white thatches of animal hair. On his bare chest hung a necklace of tiny brown animal horns and a crocodile tooth. Green palm leaves jutted vertically from split fronds tied about his waist. He walked resolutely through the circle and sat down cross-legged in its center.

"What did the spirits reveal to you?" the chief of Ilolo inquired.

He replied somberly.

"They said that there is only one kind of war stronger than this. That is white man's war. Ever since the white man arrived among us, we've seen his power with our own eyes. Do they call him 'Breaker of Stones' for nothing? When he wars, he always wins. You will win this war only if you find a way to use his power."

The men exchanged frowning glances.

"But how could we ever get his power?"

"Even if we had our houses full of wealth to pay him, would he come fight for us?"

"What wisdom do the spirits have for us? How can we lay hold of the white man's power?"

Brows were knitted. Eyes were riveted upon him.

"The strength of a man is concealed in his head. Remember for yourselves. Our forefathers performed rituals with human skulls; then they went to war and fought fearlessly. I can make the medicine you need. The spirits have given me the secret. With it you will bewitch your enemies. You will triumph over them, return to your huts, and sit in peace."

"Good! That's what we want."

"What's hindering you from making it?"

For a moment he left their question hanging in the air; then he answered.

"To make it I need the head of a white man."

Each of them sat in silence, absorbing the impact of his statement. Some faces reflected incredulity. Others frowned in deepening thought as minds struggled for a way to meet this requirement.

"How would we get the head of a white man?" asked one. "The few white men in this country are guarded with soldiers and guns."

"He may as well ask us to fell a tree with our teeth," rejoined another.

Others scorned such remarks as impertinent.

"If we fail to triumph over our enemies, don't you see our end?"

"They will keep killing us until we are subdued. Then what will our progeny say? They will hold us in shame because we despised the wisdom of the medicine man that would have saved us."

"He has revealed what we need to do. Wise men do not argue with a rooster about the time of daybreak."

They pondered in silence.

"That Baluba mission teacher who sits here in your village has a white man," one said in a sinister tone of voice. "They call him Lutonga. There are never soldiers guarding him."

"That's right," added another. "Schoolchildren say he is coming to visit in the days ahead. Let's establish the day of his arrival and have rope and weapons ready."

"That wisdom is good," the chief of Ilolo replied calmly. "But we don't want to stir up a ruckus needlessly. Lutonga has been here before. He has the habit of shaking hands with everybody. Let's build a small hut near the road. When he comes and greets us, we can lead him by the hand into the hut. Then we'll shut the door, and no one can interfere with what we need to do."

All Friday afternoon the Ilolo mission teacher was expecting the arrival of guests. Extra gourds full of water sat along the outside wall of his hut. A fresh bottle of orange palm cooking oil sat in the kitchen. It was dark now. He had just finished supper and was relaxing on a crude folding chair in his backyard. Suddenly children began yelling from the direction of the road.

"They're coming! They're coming!"

Instantaneously the cry was caught up by children across the village. They came running from all directions, combining to create a melee of joy along the roadside.

The teacher ran to join them. He noticed in the reflection of bonfires, the forms of adults quietly moving toward the road. There seemed to be more of them than customarily. Perhaps this was a good sign . . . a sign that people other than children were taking interest in the work of the mission and the message of the gospel. Yes, two lights were approaching in the road. But curiously, as they approached, he could not hear the sound of a motor. Hopes began fading, then dissipated. Two village men were returning from the forest. Each held a torch. A log they carried spaced them abreast a distance so as to stimulate auto headlights.

Suddenly in the light of the torches, the teacher recognized ominous objects in the hands of older men: knives, spears, rope. Startled, he approached them.

"I am happy when village people come to greet the white man," he said. "But this time why do you come to welcome him with weapons of war in your hands?"

They cast him furtive, menacing looks and slunk into the darkness.

Graber had found the weekend a letdown. He had planned to get away from the station for a few days and visit village Christians in the hills. An unexpected incident changed those plans so that he stayed at home. It was late Sunday afternoon. He was relaxing in the living room, thinking about what he could prepare for a light supper. Someone coughed just off the front stoop, announcing his arrival. Archie went to the front door. It was the mission teacher from the village of Ilolo.

"Life to you, teacher. Come sit down."

They shook hands and took places on veranda chairs.

"We wanted to come, like I wrote you," Graber began. "But my wife and I went for a walk to the waterfalls. She had an accident. She stumbled and hurt her leg badly. She is in bed. So our journey plans died. I know the village people were greatly saddened because we failed to come."

"Preacher, had you come, there would have been surpassing sadness. Tribal chiefs had covenanted to get your skull. They had built a hut in which to kill you. A schoolchild told me. That's why I've come all the way on foot without resting. I wanted to warn you not to come. The accident of your wife was not bad. It was good. God arranged things this way for you to escape death."

Desperate men, like hounds scenting blood, would pursue their prey to its lair. At dusk on a succeeding Sunday, a loin-skirted stranger mingled inconspicuously with Christians coming down the sloping path for an evening service at the mission station church. He was on special assignment: to secure a white man's head with which to make the fetish powerful enough to save his tribe.

Others filed into the church and left him standing outside. He took a position outside the wall, between two roof-support columns, well to the rear. The wall was chest high, and he had full view of the people and the podium. Then he waited in the gathering darkness. Their plot in the village had failed. This one would not. No one knew him here. He was a marksman. His experienced thumb checked the razor-sharp edge of a flare-bladed arrow. A single shot to the speaker's heart would do the job quickly. When people fled in terror, he would sever the head and escape into darkness..

The church was dimly lighted by kerosene lanterns set at intervals along the side walls and on the podium. It was comfortably filled. The man's eyes scanned the backs of people's heads. "Look how quietly they sit now," he mused. "In a short while their hearts will split with fear; they'll lose all their sense in fleeing to get outside. They'll remember this meeting forever." His chest swelled with the feeling of power.

A few white people came in by a side entryway and sat on front benches. Lutonga and his wife entered; he went onto the rostrum and sat down behind the pulpit. Clearly fate had decreed him as their victim. Two black leaders joined him. One rose to start the service. The stranger drew an empty bowstring and squinted across it toward the podium. There was adequate light for fixing target onto a black man; an accurate aim at Lutonga would be no problem.

The black man led them in singing. The second one rose, talked at length, and prayed. All of this was nothing to the stranger. He waited. His attention was focused only upon the work at hand. The black man ended his praying and sat down. Graber stood, took his place behind the pulput, and began to speak.

The stranger carefully seated the arrow onto the string, raised and drew the bow in a single smooth motion, and took aim. Then peculiarly, his vision fogged with a mysterious blackness. He lowered the bow; his vision cleared. Again he raised it to take aim, and again a blackish cloud concealed his target. When he lowered the bow, he could see clearly. For all the years of his life he had aimed and shot his bow at whatever his heart desired. Now, on this mission of utmost importance, which would perpetuate his name in folklore as a tribal hero, he could not see his target. Though he tried repeatedly, he was frustrated every time. He was rendered helpless, bound like a prisoner. The service ended. People exited, mingled congenially outside the church, then began moving up the path to the village, as oblivious of his presence as when they had come.

He was enraged. Then gradually his rage changed to awe, and from awe to fear. What kind of medicine did Lutonga have that he could so invoke the protection of spirits? Who were these spirits? Where did they get their power? He had wanted to kill their charge; clearly he had offended them. Were they not angry with him? They had already blinded him. Could they not kill him? He was fighting against those spirits which the medicine man said had never been defeated. He was a fool. He was defenseless before their wrath. Where did they reside? Did they fill the air around him? How could he appease them before evil befell him? Suddenly he saw the beliefs which for years had given him security swept away like a banana-leaf hut before a cyclone. Alone and abandoned, he cowered with fear.

Archie and Evelyn went home and retired. Next morning, while they were eating breakfast, Pastor Luaba and Kazadi arrived with a loin-skirted stranger. They took seats on the veranda and waited until Archie joined them. After exchanging greetings, Luaba spoke.

"This man came to church last night with an evil heart. He wanted to kill you. Every time he lifted his arrow to shoot, some spirit power blinded him. He came to me after the service. He is afraid. He knows he has done wrong."

"What do you want, my friend?" Archie asked him.

"I have offended the God of the mission. Can you show me a way to blot out my sin?"

Lutonga paused to mentally frame an answer the man could understand.

"What did your ancestors do to blot out sin? When they worshiped, they would kill a white chicken and drain its blood onto the ground. They believed that the blood would cover their sin. The Book of God tells us that God has arranged a sin offering for us. He sent us Jesus Christ, His only child. Jesus shed His blood and died, to blot out your sins. You need to tell Jesus that you are sorry for your sins. Tell Him that you are turning your heart away from the sin-way of living to follow after Him. He has promised that if you do these things, He will erase all of your sins and make you a member of His tribe. Then you won't need to be afraid any longer. God will not be angry with you. He will be your Father."

The man returned to his tribemates without a severed head, but with a strange new Presence.

7

... Poor People Make a Miracle ...

THE CHIEFS AT Ilolo were right. The white colonial government never lost a war to the black man. The colonial administrator, with black troops from the government post at Charlesville, intervened in the tribal fighting and suppressed it.

But while two related tribes demonstrated by war that they could not tolerate each other, people from a half-dozen different tribes at Charlesville were about to discover that, by combining their resources, they could triumph in a different kind of struggle.

At a weekly meeting of the church council in 1938, Pastor Luaba finished the items on his agenda. Then Lutonga asked permission to speak.

"We all see how the work of God is growing," he said. "This church building is no longer adequate. Every Sunday people come who cannot find places to sit. They stand out-of-doors and watch us across the side walls. If you have hearts to help me with some money, we can change this building into a nice big house of God."

Leaders' faces were expressionless. Their eyes scanned the church: its dimensions 100 by 40 feet; its flat dirt floor; its benches of boards nailed onto the tops of short, cut-off posts; its low brick side walls surmounted by square columns supporting bare rafters; its iron roof. It had served them well for years. It was not wearing out. It would still last for a long time. And, too, it was venerated symbol; the thought of meddling with it was too threatening. Furthermore, their minds had never grappled with a decision of such import.

61

They responded with consensus: "All the houses here have been built with money missionaries got for us. We don't know where it comes from. When they want to enlarge the church, they'll get us money for it."

"No, it is not thus," Graber protested, rising to unroll a paper plan on the floor before them. "Even in our country, when people want to build a church, they gather together money and do it. Look here." He squatted in front of them and began to trace the plan with a finger. "This part is the church as it is. We could add a large piece on this side and another large piece on that side. These big columns inside, which hold up the roof, we could take away so people can see better."

Their thinking was so uniform they didn't need to consult each other with a side-glance. A generation earlier the white man had exercised power that reduced them to slaves. Now they were in a colony under his authority. He lived among them with guns, imposing peace. He brought medicines that excelled theirs. He brought education that excelled theirs. He brought a new religion that said their gods were useless. He sold them his cast-off clothing. It was clear: all things the white man had were better than anything they possessed. They were powerless, oppressed, resourceless. They would depend upon him for everything.

One spoke for all of them. "White chief, we have hearts to help you. But why are you asking us for money? We have no money. We are poor. There is no way we can do this."

"So you are refusing to try? Do hearts that really want to help refuse to try? You already know you can't do this thing before you have even tried it? If the white man always brings you things, when will you become strong? Try to do this for yourselves. If you want to with your hearts, you can do it."

The leaders had never been confronted with such a challenge. The idea seemed entirely beyond their reach. But they discussed it and decided they would try. They told themselves that an effort would show their respect for Lutonga. And it would also confirm for them that they couldn't do it.

At a future council meeting they brought Lutonga the results of their labors . . . a few coins donated by themselves and their friends, in the bottom of a small wicker basket. To them, this was evidence enough that the project should be abandoned.

Graber stared at the coins. His face tensed. His brown eyes flashed.

"All these people who come to church every Sunday, where are they coming from?" he demanded. "God is giving them to us. Are you saying that God is giving us people, but He isn't able to give us a church for them to sit in? Does He like for us to let His people stand out in the hot sun? Don't you have shame?"

Council members were tongue-tied.

"What are you afraid of?" Lutonga pressed his advantage. "Are you saying that I do not know how to build? Who built that big office building? Who built that primary school? Who fixes up the missionary homes? Or are you saying that my word can't be trusted, that my heart will weaken and I will desert you in the middle of the work? Did you ever see me do that before? Or are you saying that I am just hunting for a way to show you that I am your big chief; I will sit idle and make you work like my slaves? Have you ever seen me do that? I will work with you as I always have, with one heart. I'll stay with you at this work from start to finish. Just accept the fact that we are going to do this thing. God will keep on showing us the way until we complete it."

Council members glanced at each other with consternation. Maybe they should reconsider. They knew that rumors of Lutonga's plan had leaked to village Christians; they had a reputation to uphold before their peers; they could not risk bearing the blame for rejecting Graber's idea. His conduct among them witnessed that his word was trustworthy. They hardly believed the project could succeed, but perhaps they could move ahead and entrust its outcome to him.

"Fathers with me," Kazadi said, "is there anything hindering us from doing what Lutonga says?"

Leaders began to reach for this impossible dream. They convened a meeting of seven overseers from the Christian village and eight area tribal chiefs. They showed them Lutonga's plan. The response was predictable.

"How could we ever do a big job like that?"

"Just like people carry an elephant carcass," mission leaders responded. "Each one bears his own share of the burden."

"Show us our share of the burden. We'll try to carry it."

"Good," the leaders replied. "The first thing you need to do is spread the news among your people of what we plan to do."

Archie later described the activities of those days. "For months there was scarcely an evening that we weren't out visiting in the villages stirring up the people. We showed them the plan and explained that each one of them could have a part in bringing it to pass. Luaba worked with the village chiefs and did a good job. But Kazadi emerged as the big pusher. Somehow the kind of life he lived gave a ring of truth to his message. He thought like a lawyer; he could see right through sham. He far excelled the other leaders as a speaker; when he spoke, people listened. He became fully convinced of the need for expanding the church. Whenever it was his turn to preach, he pushed the idea. 'This isn't the condition God's house should be in,' he would say. 'Preacher Lutonga has a plan here. We have strong bodies. We have things in our houses that we can contribute. What is hindering us from going ahead with it?' "

The church council instructed people throughout the area to prepare their donations. The project became the current topic of conversation. "What do you plan to give for building the church?" was the question in vogue. It was exchanged along footpaths, around bonfires, and across mortars hewn from tree trunks in which women pounded their flour.

Men appointed by the church council tied metal foot lockers onto their bicycle luggage-carriers. They followed preplanned itineraries and visited every home. People dropped their contributions into the metal chests: field produce, clothing, household utensils, domestic animals with their legs tied. These items were sold; the proceeds went into the "church expansion fund." Graber and other station missionaries added cash donations from their allowances.

Workmen made bricks. The first three days of the week they worked for salary; the other two days they worked for the Lord. The number of cords of wood needed to burn the bricks was prorated among the village chiefs. On a given evening criers went through villages calling out, "Tomorrow belongs to firewood! Everybody gather firewood!" On the following day chiefs forbade their people to be otherwise occupied; they went to the forest. Soon long files began emerging along the foot trails. First came the village chief; following him were his people — men, women, youths, children — all bearing on their heads burdens of firewood, often heartily singing a hymn or a traditional work chant.

There were still a few skeptics. One day a visiting missionary stood

The mission church in Charlesville after renovation *(AIMM)*

with one of the church leaders in front of the church and surveyed the fresh-dug foundations for the 24-by-24-foot wings. "Nobody should begin work like that without money in his hands," he said, "especially for a work of this size. We missionaries have never gotten together to appropriate funds for this project. Where will the money come from to finish it? Listen to me. You'll end up planting corn and sweet potatoes in those spaces. Your project will never be realized."

Kazadi later explained, "In our land, when we want a person to do something great, we don't flatter him. We reprove him. If we are hunting, and someone starts chasing an animal, we hurl insults at him. We yell after him, 'Why are you running like some old uncle? Look at that animal go! You're worthless. You'll never get it.' That stirs him up. So that missionary's word, 'You'll plant sweet potatoes there,' Stirred us up. We said, 'We'll show that man we're *not* going to plant sweet potatoes there.' From that time forward, nobody rested. Everybody — men, women, schoolchildren — worked with sweat on their bodies to help Lutonga."

Then lumber was needed, but funds were low. So every Christian was assessed the price of a board. Word of the project reached well-to-do Africans in distant cities; some were relatives of people at Charlesville; others were Christians who simply wanted to share. They sent cash contributions for lumber. Portuguese storekeepers with businesses nearby also sent their donations. An aging hunter contributed his most prized possession . . . his gun. Every Christian in the immediate area of the mission station scraped his resources to donate a board; to fail to do so would be to bear unthinkable shame. Lumber was purchased. Carpenters worked an entire month "for God."

Church leaders came to Graber with a problem. "We have to make the roof higher," they said. "Your wife, Mutekemena, has the gift of music. We want a big choir. As the roof is now, if a big choir wants to stand up in front, their heads will hit the rafters. We're building a nice church. Can't we have a sufficient place for the choir to stand? We want to lift the roof."

Their enthusiasm had picked up such momentum that Graber couldn't bear to disappoint them. He found two jackscrews. With them he lifted the rafter off the first wall-support column along one side; then he inserted two layers of loose brick, and lowered the rafter onto them. He directed workmen to follow the same procedure for each of the remaining fifteen columns in turn, going around the building once. The roof was now raised four inches. They repeated the process until by circuiting the building nine times, they had lifted the roof a total of three feet. Then Graber blocked the roof with lumber props and built arches between the original columns to support it.

The community worked at the project for eighteen months and completed it. On dedication day the church was packed. The people, looking about them, absorbed the full impact of their labors. They were exuberant.

They sat on wooden benches with backs. Under their feet a brick floor sloped toward the front. Over their heads was a board ceiling. No interior support columns obstructed their view. A new brick parapet around the edge of the rostrum was decorated with a border of pomegranates molded in concrete and hand-painted. Up on the rostrum stood a new, dark, hardwood pulpit; and on the floor in front of it, a matching Communion table with the words *Do this in remembrance of me* inlaid in ivory on its front face.

Behind the pulpit was a semicircular choir loft with three rows of tiered seats, accommodating 104 people. In the center of the circular wall above the top tier of seats was a long, blue scroll formed of concrete, with raised white letters saying, "Hold fast until I come . . . Rev. 2:25." In the center of the blue scroll was an open Bible with a cross and a crown lying across the pages.

Church leaders had prepared a program befitting the occasion. It is natural for the African to express his joy by means of music. The congregation sang with exhilaration. Groups visiting from great distances brought special musical numbers. The full choir sang its anthems. Interspersed through the program were speakers with appropriate words commemorating the event. Africans insisted that Graber open the account books to dispel any suspicion of misappropriation of mission funds and to prove they had completed the project using local resources. Then at last, they gave final vent to their joy in singing "Christ the Lord Is Risen Today."

Someone says, "They built a church. So what?"

African Christians from Charlesville give this experience highest priority. One says, "Never in the history of Charlesville before or after was there anything like it, the way people gave themselves with one heart to accomplish such work." For the participants, something happened to self-image. In that experience there was resurrected in the lives of hundreds of people an awareness of self-worth and resourcefulness which would never leave them the same, and which someday would serve them well in a context they could not now imagine.

8

... Malevolent Plot ...

FOR MANY PEOPLE living in the Charlesville "Christian village," the benefits enjoyed from the church expansion project were alloyed by a besetting rumor of a growing power struggle between church leaders. It had long aggravated the church body as a persistent inflammation; now it threatened to break into an open sore.

One bright Sunday morning after breakfast Archie heard subdued voices off his front doorstep. He glanced out the door and saw two men, Kazadi and Ngalula, both teachers in the Bible school. He went out the door to meet them. A band of brilliant, multicolored zinnias in the veranda flower boxes caught his eye; how many ways did Evelyn's love for beauty grace their home!

"Life to you," Graber greeted the men. "Come, sit down."

They mounted the steps, stooped slightly to clear the leaves of the bougainvillea vine rambling along the roof edge, and took seats on the veranda. "Why are they so somber?" Graber wondered. It made their black faces appear even darker.

"Preacher," Kazadi began, "you missionaries came with the Word of God. You told us about Christ. We believed your words. We left behind us our sin-way of living. We entered a new family. You are our parents. You gave birth to us. A proverb of our ancestors says, 'Correct the ways of your own children; then orphans you feed will correct theirs.' If a child is breaking the rules of the family, and his evil conduct is ruining the family reputation before outsiders, what should the parent do?"

"The parent should reprimand him."

"If the offender is an older child and is hiding his evil from the parents, is it good for younger children to be silent?"

"No. It is good for a parent to know the conduct of his children."

"We have not come to see you for nothing. Our hearts are weighted with great heaviness. If we don't show you this matter, someday ahead you will grieve sorely, and we will look like undependable children. Everybody in the village is murmuring about it. Our elder in the work of Christ, the one whom we all ought to respect, is trying to annihilate us."

Graber could recall incidents that suggested Pastor Luaba might be jealous of them, but he dismissed the thought that Luaba might want actually to do them evil. He understood something of African traditional religion. Natives believed that the world about them was filled with malevolent spirits. For the most part, their religion was comprised of rites designed to appease and control these spirits. Africans' constant fear of being victims of spiritual malevolence gave them a low threshold of suspicion. In all probability, Archie reasoned, Kazadi and Ngalula were building a case upon incidental circumstances.

"When did you first see that he had a bad heart toward you?"

"When you missionaries began talking about ordaining additional church leaders. He does not want to share his position with another person."

"How do you know that he wants to kill you?"

"We have seen signs of it for a long time, but we did not tell you," Kazadi continued. "Now it has become clear. Do you remember when we went to annual conference? We were in the church. The delegates approved that our friend Kamba and I be ordained to become assistant pastors. Then there was a hard thunderstorm. Lightning struck just outside the church. We saw the bolt. People's hearts split with fear. They wanted to flee outside. In a few days you missionaries forgot about it. But we did not. That lightning did not strike for nothing. Luaba was not in that meeting. He had paid a medicine maker of the area to throw a lightning bolt to kill Kamba and me. Witnesses there established the truth of this. But because we were innocent, the bolt failed to hit us."

Archie along with missionaries in general surmised that Africans accorded medicine makers credit they did not always deserve; but black Christians were convinced such persons had supernatural power to inflict harm. "You white people say that such a bolt comes from electricity in the clouds, but we don't accept that," they would say. "We who are born in this country have confirmed that such bolts are sent by spiritual powers who obey a medicine maker."

"Have you seen other signs that Luaba wants to do you evil?" Graber asked.

"When rains began at the end of last dry season," Kazadi continued, "a lightning bolt struck my house. Don't you remember? In all the years I have sat here, nothing like that ever happened before. What about the time a lightning bolt struck the church and killed the son of another of our leaders? We had to diligently guard the corpse because medicine makers wanted to come and take its tongue; don't you recall? And this morning, when Ngalula left his house, in the footpath, buried where he would step on it, he discovered a chicken egg. This is the work of a witch doctor. Had Ngalula stepped on that egg, he would have been cursed. Don't you see the mind of Luaba toward us church leaders?"

Mentally Graber began to concede that someone was engaged in activities inappropriate for a Christian village, but he was unwilling to attribute them to Luaba.

"You say that people in the village are talking about it. What are they saying?"

Kazadi glanced at him and paused, reluctant to continue. Ngalula spoke.

"Preacher, at first their words were like any of the breezes that stir the leaves. But then you remember what happened that Sunday in church when Luaba was preaching. The big snake crawled up the inside wall; everybody saw it. People fled from the church in dismay, they stayed outside until someone killed it. That sign convinced everybody that Luaba is guilty. People all remember that long ago, when the Bakuba chief, Djoko Punda, gave this land to the mission, he and other chiefs declared that it was to be hallowed perpetually. No one, ever, was to live on it with a heart to kill or to do another evil by sorcery. He, a pagan chief, used his authority to make a path for the work of God to go forward. Most of us sitting here are not native to this land; Djoko Punda allows us to sit here as guests. Now the black leader of the mission work from another tribe, who sits here as a guest, uses the sorcery of pagans to destroy the work of God. It is a matter of great shame. People are left weak. In their hearts they have rejected Luaba. They hold him in contempt."

Graber was stunned. He had known Pastor Luaba for years. He recalled the farewell service in the church when he and his wife, who was in poor health, had left for furlough. Groups with whom they had worked closely — students, teachers, workmen — sang songs especially composed for the occasion, which expressed their esteem for Lutonga and Mutekemena. Numerous people in the congregation gave spontaneous testimonies of their love. An atmosphere of warm comradeship developed which was deep and touching. Then Pastor Luaba had risen and asked Graber and his wife, "If the Lord supplies your needs and removes obstacles from your path, do you promise before this church by lifting your hands that you will come back to us?" They raised their hands. He turned to the congregation and said, "Will you promise before our missionaries by lifting your hands that you will be true to what they have taught you while they have been among us?" Hundreds raised their hands.

Could it be that this man himself was now untrue?

Once, Archie recalled, he and Luaba had gone down the hill from the station to the river for a baptismal service. They had found large crowds waiting on both sides of the river. Graber remembered commenting to Luaba how encouraging it was to see such a large number of people show interest in the work of the church. When they had finished baptizing and walked onto shore, a fight broke out in the crowd ahead of them. They later learned that enemies of Luaba had paid a witch doctor to pour medicine into the river upstream which would cause a crocodile to attack Luaba while he stood in the water. Word had circulated, and the crowd had gathered to see it happen. When it didn't, the conspirators assaulted the witch doctor and demanded repayment of their fee. Graber asked Luaba, "If you had known that they had put medicine in the water to take your life, would you have gone into the water to work with me?" Luaba had replied, "Preacher, the Lord who saved my soul from sin could keep back that crocodile from taking my life. I would have baptized with you."

Had this dedicated pastor now, himself, become a malicious collaborator with the forces of darkness for the purpose of murder?

Graber turned his attention back to the men sitting beside him.

"You, as leaders of the church, what do you think we should do?"

"Don't you see that so long as we let him continue unhindered, our lives and the lives of our children are in jeopardy?" asked Kazadi.

"Who will the medicine man try to kill next?"

"The church council must call Luaba and require him to give account of his conduct," added Ngalula. "One rancid caterpillar spoils the whole panful. This affair has weakened the arms of all the Christians. If we are silent, it will ruin the whole church."

Archie's mind was in a quandry. It was his nature to have great faith in people. He found it difficult to impute evil motives to anyone professing loyalty to Christ. Plus, Luaba was an ordained minister. For years, from the church pulpit and in the villages, he had publicly affirmed his Christian faith. On countless occasions, under his influence people had destroyed their fetishes, renounced their allegiance to sin, and responded to his appeal to follow Jesus. Graber had learned to love this black brother deeply and to trust him completely.

But Archie also loved Kazadi and Ngalula, and to openly defend Luaba before them would be to impugn their integrity. Would these two men possibly fabricate such accusations to promote jealous ambition? If so, Luaba would surely label such remarks as talebearing and would use them as evidence that his colleagues harbored ill intentions toward him. Who was out to get whom? Where was the path of truth in the matter? Which of these brethren was concealing treachery beneath a cloak of trustworthiness?

"You have done well to come and tell me," Archie responded. "Perhaps we will need to talk the matter over in church council. But this is a weighty affair. If we talk it over in the church council now, we will throw wood onto the fire. First, I want to try to understand the heart of Luaba. Sometimes the word of a friend can help a person; the words of a group may drive him away. Entrust yourselves into the hands of Christ alone. We missionaries will be praying for you that He will protect you and your families. Now before you go, let's pray and lay this burden in front of God."

9

... Wooing a Prodigal ...

A FRIEND WHO betrays one's love and trust inflicts a cruel wound. Persons who have experienced such betrayal would probably agree with Archie and Evelyn that few wounds are more painful. If such betrayal is quickly exposed, the wound can be treated and healed. On the other hand, covert betrayal can become a hemorrhaging wound, compelling one to live with irremediable weakness.

The Grabers and other missionaries close to Pastor Luaba endured the different forms of pain which are part of such an experience. First, there is incredulity. Events unfold that cause emotions to vacillate between hope and disillusionment. Then comes the exposure that others are caught in the web of evil. Such exposure brings distress. All the while, a person struggles to maintain equal faith in two antagonistic parties, one or the other of which is apparently living in calculated deceit. Eventually guilt is established. One resigns himself to the truth of the matter but afterwards hesitates to place faith in anyone, lest its betrayal again cause such pain.

Such were the currents that swirled around the person of Pastor Luaba. With the passing of months, they rose and fell and rose again. They sucked in an unsightly assortment of debris. On the basis of accumulating circumstantial evidence, Luaba was eventually relieved of his pastoral duties. He stopped coming to church.

Once Archie told a newly arrived missionary, "If you've come for the glamour of it, that will wear off real fast. Times will come when you are so discouraged that only the call of God will hold you here." For

Graber, surely this was such a time. But he had observed the faithfulness of Luaba for too many years to think that Christ was done with him now. Communications remained open between them; they visited each other frequently. But Luaba refused to acknowledge any wrongdoing.

Graber had a black friend who, he felt, was closer to him than a brother. He was a spiritual giant, a man of prayer, whose quiet life seemed to effuse the power of God. He had a great love for the church, a deep concern for its people, and sought to keep abreast of affairs in the spiritual community to make them matters of personal prayer. Early one Sunday morning Archie made his way to this man's home. It was Graber's turn to preach that day; burdened about Luaba, he coveted this man's counsel and prayers.

He walked up the path to the first street of the Christian village and approached his friend's hut. Thatch on its roof was gray and weatherbeaten; dirt on its walls was crumbling, exposing portions of their rattan framework. The door was open. He stooped low to peer inside.

"Life to you, Dikuki."

"Preacher Lutonga. Life to you. Enter."

The hut's single, windowless room was about seven feet square. From the far right corner a setting hen eyed the visitor suspiciously. In the center of the dirt floor were the fragile white ashes of a night fire. Above the spot was suspended a bamboo rack, black with baked tar from countless fires and bearing a burden of dry, brown, unhusked corn. Between the fire and the right wall were a sturdy, brown wooden box worn shiny from sitting and a wicker chair warped from long use. On the left, extending from the far wall, a crude screen of woven palm leaf, gray and brittle with age, partitioned off a narrow portion of the room. Exposed to view past the near end of the partition was the end of a low, crude, bamboo-frame platform which served as a bed. It was covered with a worn gray blanket from which protruded two black feet.

Archie entered the hut, reached behind the partition into the semidarkness to shake a thin, deformed hand, and sat down on the end of the bed.

"My friend, I am sorry to see you lying down. Are you ill?"

"No, preacher. As you know, war wounds from when I was a soldier long ago left my body as it is. Now on top of that, old age is beginning to afflict me. Tell me, what's going on in the village?"

"My heart is greatly burdened for Luaba. People cannot keep still.

Their gossip is like a poisoned water-spring. They keep adding new things on top of the old. The affair is weakening the whole church. Accusations that we hear, are they true or false? Luaba and I still visit each other. He denies any wrongdoing. I tell him that when he refuses to come to church, people say that proves he is guilty. He says he will not come sit in his place in church when he knows everybody's eyes are on him. I am to preach this morning. What shall I say to help the people? What wisdom can I follow to draw Luaba back into the right path?''

Graber's eyes had adjusted now to the darkness, so that he could see Dikuki's form. The old man was propped up on one elbow, deep in thought, framing a response.

"Like rain beating on a dirt wall, so gossip reduces its victim to a worthless thing. People's accusations make him feel like a discarded rag. Maybe he has done bad things; maybe he has not. If we keep trying to prove his guilt, we are wasting our strength. We are driving him away. He must understand that even though he may have failed, he is a person of worth. He must believe that God still loves him, people care about him, his place in the church is still waiting for him, there is still work for him to do, and there is no obstacle in the way of his returning.''

Archie recognized these as wise and temperate words. They gave him insight for his morning message.

"Thank you, my friend. We want to pray; then I will go. And when I am preaching this morning, remember me before God.''

"Before you leave," Dikuki interrupted, "I want to ask you about something.''

"What is it?''

"This crippled body of mine is getting weaker. For me to get around with my walking stick like I once did is very hard. You know how I like to visit people in their homes, and talk with them about the Lord, and pray with them. My heart goes out to them. They need my help. Can you not arrange some way for me to get around?''

"I want to help you. I'll hunt for a way.''

They prayed together, and the missionary left. How can it be, Graber mused, that God uses a poor, crippled, unlettered man to be an instrument of such consolation and strength? Then he remembered a couple of junked wheelbarrows. He would salvage the wheels, use a length of galvanized pipe for an axle, mount a sturdy box with a tongue on it, and paint it nicely. Schoolchildren would pull it. Dikuki would have a way to get around. You bet he would! A pull-cart in which he would take as much pride as any millionnaire does in his Rolls Royce.

Graber went home and prepared his message. The bell rang a last time, anncouncing the start of the service. He went to the church and took his place behind the pulpit. The building was packed. The hundred-voice choir sang a special number. Then Graber read the account of King Herod's execution of John the Baptist (Matt. 14:1-12). While Evelyn played her guitar and sang a song calling the wayward, Archie drew a colored chalk sketch of John's decapitated head on a platter. Then he began to preach. His deep emotions almost overwhelmed him. He heard his voice rise in plaintive appeal. His mood gripped the audience. People sat motionless, their eyes fastened on him. What followed is best described by a black man who was there:

"Lutonga explained that John the Baptist kept reminding Herod of his sin. Herod did not want to be made ashamed. So he cut off the head of John, uselessly. The words coming from Lutonga's mouth brought Lutonga himself to a point of great sorrow. His eyes spilling tears, he cried out, 'Luaba, where are you? Do you want to be like Herod? You are a person of renown. You don't want to share your honor with another. People love you. They want to help you. They see that you have erred. You are afraid of enduring shame. And so you want to catch people whom you fear. You want to cut their heads off, for nothing. Look at the place where you customarily sit. It is still empty. Who is taking your place? We haven't deserted you. God hasn't deserted you. The church needs you. It is waiting for you to return. Why do we hear that you long to put the heads of God's people onto a platter?' At that moment nobody in the church had bad thoughts about anybody. Everyone hearing Lutonga's words came to understand his love for Luaba and they wept with him."

Graber went home, ate lunch, and was taking an afternoon nap when there was a cough at the front veranda. He got up and went to the door.

"Pastor Luaba. Come sit down."

They took chairs on the veranda and talked casually for awhile until Luaba found a way to approach his subject.

"During these months I have been carrying a great burden," he said. "People have been maligning me. My own relatives have renounced me. I began to feel that there was not a single person among the blacks or whites who cared about me any more. But today, people came from church and related to me your words. You say that the church needs me. You say that my place there still remains vacant. I still have strength to work for God. But first I need to confess that I've touched evil things, which cling like mud to my fingers. I wanted to obstruct people's plans. So I made ancestral medicine, wanting to kill them. I have consorted with powers of evil. I wanted to show my strength. I wanted to show that there was no one who could challenge me. I would do something which would shake heaven and earth. But God has shown me today that His power is stronger. He has shown me the evil of my way and told me to come talk with you. I want to clean my hands. I want to rid myself of this burden. I want to take my place in church again.''

10

... Stretching Old Wineskins ...

MBUYI, THE GOATHERD, had no spectacular gifts. He was illiterate. He never preached a sermon; he never sang in public; he was never asked to serve on the church council. He was not attractive, his frame was short and spare, with the passing of years his ready smile became increasingly toothless, and his pock-marked face was strikingly etched with deep wrinkles. But he continued unswervingly loyal to Christ, to the work of the mission, and to the Grabers.

For several years he was the mission goatherd. He and his wife lived in a hut just off Graber's backyard, so he served, also, as night sentinel for the Graber residence. Then he was promoted to mail carrier; he was given a uniform — a blue-denim jacket with four square pockets and brass buttons, a pair of matching shorts, and a maroon felt fez. For many years, he made twice-weekly round trips on foot with the mailbag to the post office forty miles away; he made periodic mail trips to other mission stations fifty or more miles distant.

Over the years he routinely met the obligations of these varying kinds of mission work. He was paid a modest salary. Then, in the early forties, he and his wife were confronted with a different kind of challenge — one that would reveal to them a hitherto-unknown gift and bring them returns greater than money could buy. It stemmed from a crisis that developed in the Graber household.

It was getting dark one evening when Evelyn called Archie into the bedroom. She was bending over the body of a ten-year-old black boy, her hand on his brow.

"Tshiamalenga's fever isn't breaking," she said gravely. "You'd better put the other children to bed. I'll probably have to stay up with him again tonight."

As Graber carried out the duties of a father, he recalled the curious sequence of events which had brought them an adopted family. On his recurring trips through outlying villages, he had become well acquainted with the mission's evangelist-teachers who lived in them. One such person contracted tuberculosis. Graber observed the man's increased suffering as the disease progressed. On a final visit, when it was apparent that death was near, the sick man asked Graber to take responsibility for raising his two small sons, Tshiamalenga and Kalubi. Archie and Evelyn loved children, though they had none of their own. They felt that by honoring the dying man's request they could broaden their ministry. So they took the children.

On a later trip into a different tribal area, Archie had come upon two orphan boys who had no known relatives and who faced the prospect of slow death from neglect. He took Dikenga and Ituma home with him. Then another evangelist-teacher died, leaving his oldest son, Mamba, in Archie's custody. Now Archie and Evelyn had a family of five boys. They could provide the love of parents and the security of a home until the children entered their teens. After that the boys could make their own way as students in the mission boarding school. Caring for the children had come to be a heavy responsibility. But what enrichment the young boys had brought into their lives!

Archie put the other four children to bed, brought Evelyn a more comfortable chair, and seated himself in the bedroom with her. Silence was broken only by the listless child's labored breathing, his periodic coughing, and the ticking of a clock on the dresser. At 10:00 P.M. Evelyn inserted a thermometer in the boy's mouth, waited, removed it, and studied it closely in the light of a kerosene lamp on the bedstand.

"It says 104," she said. "The antimalarial medicine the nurse gave him at six o'clock hasn't done a thing. If his fever goes much higher, he'll go into convulsions. We'd better start sponge-bathing him to see if we can bring it down."

Archie brought a basin, cloths, and a bottle of water from a primitive cold box. As he watched his wife work, he began to sense the depth of his attachment to the child. Why is it, he thought, that in a time of crisis, the child who has caused you the most frustration seems to be the one you love the most? Tshiamalenga was small for his age. His father, because of prolonged illness, has been unable to provide an adequate living for his family; and so Tshiamalenga's growth from the outset had been slowed by malnutrition. To allay the pangs of hunger, the young boy had taken to stealing — a habit he was now loathe to forsake, even though his basic needs were met.

But Tshiamalenga did not mean to be disobedient. He had responded more quickly to their loving care than any of the others. His body had fleshed out; he had become an attractive child, with deep dark eyes and a bright ready smile. In those first years, when he wanted something, he had a way of wrapping his hand around one of Archie's big fingers, looking up with expectant, happy eyes, and saying "my father" in a manner virtually irresistible.

Archie's thoughts were interrupted by a stirring on the bed. Dry, husky coughing racked the boy's body. Evelyn slipped an arm beneath him for support; the spasm subsided. Then she laid his head back onto the pillow.

"What makes him cough like that?" Archie asked.

"There is always a lot of coughing among the Africans toward the end of dry season. It's probably because there is so much dust in the air. But for a lot of people, it goes into pneumonia, too."

"Do you really think he'll make it?" He didn't need to fear asking the question; the boy could not understand English.

"The Lord knows. If only we'd have learned earlier that he has intestinal parasites. He could have taken medicine to get rid of them before he came down with this sickness. But he's too weak for that now. All we can do is pray."

That was true. They could not go to bed. They could not divert their attention to some other useful activity. All they could do was pray. Periodically Archie would rise, go to the cold box, bring some fresh water, and return to his chair; then he would resume praying. Evelyn continued tenderly stroking the cool cloths over the black body; occasionally she took the boy's temperature. Finally she studied the thermometer, turned to Archie and spoke.

"It's down to 101. I think the crisis is past for now. Why don't you go to bed and get some rest? I'll probably be coming pretty soon."

The clock on the dresser said 1:30. Graber went to bed and slept uneasily until daybreak.

As Evelyn continued to care for Tshiamalenga day by day, he made a steady recovery. But nursing him back to health had demanded much. That, added to her regular duties of teaching in the Bible school, conducting choir rehearsals, and caring for her family left her exhausted. She contracted a cough, came down with a fever, and was bedfast for several weeks. Archie's own program of daily responsibilities was disrupted while he attended to family duties and nursed his wife through a slow recovery.

Then one morning, when they were finishing breakfast, they heard a cough at the door of the breezeway joining the house to the kitchen. Archie rose, went to the door, and found a sad-faced stranger, whose lean body was sparsely covered with the tatters of mourning. In his arms he carried a tiny baby girl with spindly, drawn limbs.

After Archie greeted him, the man launched into his story:

"Preacher, I am a person of great sorrow. From the time my wife and I entered marriage, our hearts yearned for a child. When she failed to conceive, my relatives urged me to discard her and marry someone else. But I am a Christian. I refused their counsel. After five years, God heard our cries and she became pregnant. We had surpassing joy while we awaited the birth of our child. But when the time for birth came, she had trouble. Our village is far from here; there was no one to help her. God took her soul and left me with the child. I have tried to take care of it, but there is no one with milk for it. Since it was born three days ago, I have been feeding it sweet palm wine. It is not growing; it is getting weaker. It is my only child, borne me by the wife I loved. I watched my wife die. I don't want to see my child die. So I came with it here. Will you please keep it at your house and give it the milk it needs? Keep it as your own child, so its life is saved."

Archie's heart reached out to help the man. At the same time, he was keenly aware of the family burden they were already carrying.

"First, sit down," he said, motioning toward a wicker chair near the outside house wall. "I need to talk with my wife."

He returned to his chair at the breakfast table and explained the situation to Evelyn. She went out to see the infant and returned.

"That little baby will surely die if we don't help," she said. "We can't turn the man away."

"There's no question about that," Archie replied. "But I think you're already trying to do too much. The burden you're carrying now is wearing you down. You can't take upon yourself all the work that goes with caring for another orphan. Can't we provide for the baby's needs somehow without actually taking it into our home?"

"How can we arrange something like that?" she asked.

Archie pondered, restlessly drumming his fingers on the table.

"Why don't we find a place for the man to live here in the Christian village?" he suggested. "If the father loves that baby, he'll be happy to bring it here whenever it needs feeding. Our cook can warm the milk and prepare the bottle."

Evelyn's serious face registered disapproval.

"Archie, an infant needs more than milk. It needs loving care. It needs these things not only for a few months but for years. If the father moves here to care for the child, he will need to eat. This means he will have to plant fields and care for them. When he has to leave home day after day to work in his fields, what will he do with the baby? How can a child growing up this way know what the love of a home is all about?"

"You yourself know that if I turned that baby away knowing it will die, I would not sleep well at night," he replied. "But the Lord has given us our bodies, and I think He expects us to take care of them. We can take the baby into our home for now. But let's be praying that there will be some way for us to cope with this added burden."

The father gave them his baby, thanked them profusely, and left. Evelyn nursed and cared for the infant as if it were her own. Archie tried to lighten her duties during the evening and night hours when he was at home; but when he left the house after early breakfast each morning, the picture of her wan face drawn with lines of fatigue lingered in his thinking. She endured her prolonged weakness with stoic resignation, but it drained her of joy. In what alternative manner could they provide the care the baby needed? Archie and Evelyn kept it for three weeks. Then one afternoon while working on a construction project, an idea occurred to Archie that he could hardly wait to share with his wife.

"Evelyn, come here," he called as he came into the house that evening. He sat down at the dining room table. He would tell her before he took time to clean up for supper. She came from the side of the crib in the bedroom and joined him.

"You know, we've been asking the Lord to show us how this baby can be properly cared for without adding to the work load we're already carrying. I think He gave me the answer today."

"What do you think He wants us to do?"

"Mbuyi and his wife, Delela, live right next to us here. They have no children. They are warm-hearted, quiet people. They would make good parents. They have a lot of love to give to an orphaned child."

She smiled cautiously. "That would certainly be something new for them. After we eat, let's call them and see what they say."

Archie and Evelyn gathered their children around the table and ate supper. Then Archie placed chairs in the screened passageway toward the kitchen and called Mbuyi to come with his wife. They came and took seats. Archie noted Mbuyi's small, spare body, knobby knees, sinewy legs, and calloused feet. He wondered if his black friend who had served them well as a goatherd, a sentry, and a mailman would now be ready to begin assuming the role of a father.

"Mbuyi, you and Delela have been Christians for a long time. You know the teachings of God's Book. What should we do when we find someone suffering?"

"We should help him," Mbuyi answered automatically.

"We have seen in your land that people leave orphaned children to suffer. Jesus said that children are precious; He does not want them to suffer. My wife, Mutekemena, and I have tried to help them. That's why we have taken five of them into our home. We count them as our own children. They bring us much joy."

The black man and woman were listening intently.

"In our land, friends sent us to school to learn how to help people here," Graber continued. "We learned how to preach the Bible, how to teach people to sing, how to construct buildings. We came to live among you, and we are doing these things. A few days past, another suffering child was brought to us. Our hands are full of work. If we take time to care for another child, we will be hindered from doing the kinds of work we were trained to do. We have thought hard about this problem. We have prayed for God to give us wisdom. Then we remembered about you and Delela."

They hadn't shifted their eyes from him. They were puzzled, but the gravity of his words commanded their patience.

"You and Delela have been our friends for a long time," Lutonga continued. "You are Christians. You have good hearts. As with Mutekemena and me, God has not given you children of your own. You have had no opportunity to go to school to learn how to help others. But you can love a little child. If you take this little girl, we will share the burden; we will give you milk and clothing for her. But you can keep her at your house and count her as your own child. That way you will make Jesus happy. You will help us. And you will save the life of a person. This is a way you can work for God. What do you think?''

The little man looked down at his folded hands. His brow wrinkles deepened as he pondered the situation and slowly framed his reply.

''Preacher Lutonga, you know since the day you arrived, I have never refused your word. But what you are asking us to do now is a difficult matter. You know how it is among us. Tribemates never cease to taunt me saying, 'Your wife is a dead stick. What has she given you?' Now if we take an orphan, they will say, 'Are you trying to deceive us? That is somebody else's child.' You yourself know that when the child is old enough to begin school, classmates will scorn her. They'll say, 'That man and woman caring for you are not your parents; someone else gave birth to you.' We'll run into all kinds of problems.''

''All parents have problems,'' Archie replied. ''Whether you bear a child of your own, or whether you raise the child of someone else, the day a little one enters your home, that day you will begin to have problems. But when a man and a wife enter into marriage, they don't say, 'We refuse to bear children; they will bring us problems.' The man and wife receive children with great joy. When a problem comes, they find wisdom to deal with it. We are here to help you. Have we ever let you down any other time? We'll support you. When problems come, we'll help you with them. And don't fear the thinking of your tribemates. You are a Christian; you know such thinking is wrong. If you wanted to get up in church and teach people, they would not respect you because you have not been to school. But if you took an orphan child for your own, and loved it as Jesus does, they would respect you. You would teach them a powerful lesson that would help to bring their thinking into the right path.''

There was a glimmer of light in the man's face as if he were almost convinced; then as he weighed the cost, it died.

''I want to talk over this matter with Delela,'' he replied. ''We will answer you later.'' They rose to leave.

''Go well,'' Graber said, putting a hand on the man's shoulder. ''God go with you.''

It was difficult for Archie and Evelyn to drop off to sleep that night.

Bible school students with (left to right, front) Ngalula, Luaba, and Kazadi *(WCC)*

Mbuyi

They were praying. Mbuyi and Delela stood on the edge of great discovery. To the missionaries, this thought was more exciting than the prospect of their own reduced work load.

Shortly after Archie arose next morning, Mbuyi was at the door.

"Preacher, we didn't sleep well last night. We talked this business over for a long time. If you promise to stand with us and help us with all the problems that come up in the years ahead, we'll take the child."

African parents are characteristically reserved about openly expressing love. But bonds of love which began tying together the members of this new family were soon apparent. Three times a day Delela brought the baby to the Graber's house, got a bottle of warm milk, then sat in the screened passageway and fed her. Frequently Evelyn would observe Delela seated on a low stool outside her hut with her back half-turned, coddling the baby with the warmth and fulfillment of any new mother. Mbuyi took his turn after work at night, when he would sit contentedly at an outside bonfire cradling the infant in his arms.

Love, fostered by their care for the child, began to give their lives a new dimension of sensitivity and concern. Gradually they became less dependent on the Grabers for the material needs of the child. About three years later they took responsibility for the care of a second orphaned girl. They were discovering within themselves a reserve of love that others needed. and in sharing it, they found joy.

Archie and Evelyn were happy to see that Mbuyi and Delela were providing the children with a happy home. In the context of black African culture, this in itself was unusual. Permanent adoption was something else. It was so rare that no civil procedures existed to legalize it. The Grabers were praying that their friends would take the much more difficult step of publicly and permanently claiming the children as their own. Eventually the matter presented itself in the unexpected form of a problem.

It was after supper. Mbuyi came to the door of the screened porch. He wanted to talk. Graber brought two chairs from the dining room. Mbuyi came in and they sat down.

"Preacher, these two girl-children of mine are still small. Their parents are no longer here; but I know there are a lot of relatives who know where they are living. Our forefathers said, 'People are greedy; like a partridge, they scratch with ten fingers at once." People don't want the trouble of caring for an orphaned relative; but when she is grown, they are proud to tell everyone she is their child. When our girls approach puberty, their relatives will appear to claim them. As you know, a father's wealth is in his daughters. When they marry, they bring him bride price. When the time comes, relatives will appear, take our girls, marry them off, and put the bride prices into their pockets. We are working hard to teach these girls the things of God. We don't want them to marry pagans. What will we do the day relatives come to claim them?''

"What you say is true," Graber replied. "Relatives of the older boy we are raising came to take him. I sat down and made a list of all the money I had spent on his food and clothing. Year after year, it comes to a big number. I told them to reimburse me the money I spent on the child, and then they could take him. They never returned."

"You can do that way because you are a white man," Mbuyi explained. "We black people are afraid to enter into dispute with a white man. But I am black. If I do that way, the children's relatives will take me to court. Our laws respect birth lineage. The white-man judge will ask me, if I have truly taken care of the children these many years, why did I never inform him? He will honor the appeal of the relatives and give them the children. To escape such trouble, I need to arrange the matter now while the children are still young."

"You have lived here for a long time," Graber responded. "The white government man across the river knows you well; he's seen you pass his office with your uniform and the mailbag many times. You and Delela should go with your children and see him tomorrow morning. You should have their names written into your tax book to show that you are their parents. I'll write a letter for you to give him. When morning comes, I'll call Pastor Kazadi to go with you. When the girls grow up, and your tax book shows that you have been caring for them for many years, their relatives will find no way of taking them."

"That's good," Mbuyi said, his face lighting with his affirmation. "Then the children will remain in my name forever."

11

... Forging the Bonds
of Friendship ...

CHRISTIANS READILY identify when Bunyan describes Pilgrim's struggle with that hideous monster Apollyon. Most believers, like Pilgrim, though wounded by Apollyon's darts and pressed unto death, recover from his assaults and resume their pilgrimages the stronger. But such was not the case with Pastor Luaba. The forces of darkness engaged him in a prolonged seesaw war until eventually he became gravely ill, made a final confession of sin, and died in 1952.

Consequently Pastor Kazadi carried growing responsibility in the national church and gradually emerged as its leading figure. Increasingly, this brought him into close contact with Graber, who was himself responsible for nurturing the church in villages throughout the region assigned to the Charlesville mission. Difficult experiences they shared together forged strong bonds of friendship and of mutual appreciation, bonds that proved crucial at a later point in their lives.

The Kasai River flows eastward past Charlesville and soon thereafter turns left. It follows this northerly course for just over a hundred miles, then bows westward and forms the northern geographic limit of the Charlesville field. There, on its south bank, lay a thriving commercial center and an important government outpost called Basonga. Adjacent to Basonga westward, and blanketing the undulating hills along the river for twenty-five miles, was a palm-oil plantation. It provided oil for a British corporation known as Lever Brothers, it operated under the heavy thumb of the Belgian colonial government and was called Brabanta.

Employment opportunities in the various enterprises of this area drew a large heterogeneous tribal population. Families of over a thousand employees lived in workmen's camps dispersed throughout the palm plantation. The population of Basonga approached three thousand. Africans in traditional village settings existed on a subsistence level. But most people living in the Basonga–Brabanta area were wage earners who had financial resources they could devote to the work of the Lord. Many of the tribesmen taking leading positions in these enterprises were aggressive Baluba; some among them were Christians. They were evolving into a class of social elite. Christian employees and their families, uprooted and displaced from their diverse tribal settings, found a sense of cohesion in their common faith. They were committed. And so this field held the potential of great growth for the church of Christ.

But there was a problem. The Catholic party controlling the government in Belgium sought to control also the social structure of its distant African colony. In the hinterland of what was then known as Belgian Congo, the welcome winds of Vatican II had not yet begun to rustle. The convention signed by the Belgian government and the British Lever Brothers corporation gave the Catholic church exclusive rights for social and spiritual ministry to the company workers; and these rights were zealously defended by members of the Catholic mission established at Brabanta.

Protestant evangelist-teachers from Charlesville built a mission outpost at Basonga. From there they preached in surrounding villages. They made periodic incursions into Brabanta, worshiping surreptitiously with believers from among the plantation workers. Archie and Evelyn looked forward to their trips to visit this northern area at least once a year; but each time they braced themselves for the insults and hostility the work there had to endure.

In February 1938, they traveled north all day and arrived at the southwestern limit of the Brabanta plantation in late afternoon. "We were not allowed to hold a service with the workers there," Evelyn later wrote home. "We weren't even to stay there overnight. The local authorities did not want us to put a teacher in their village, and even tried to stop our putting a teacher in a chief's village (outside the plantation) nearby." [1] And so they continued their journey another twenty miles

[1]*Congo Missionary Messenger,* July-August 1938, p. 12.

east to Basonga, where they were warmly welcomed by the people and were tolerated by the local white government authority.

Brabanta Protestant families could worship freely at Basonga. Regularly on weekends, they came on foot for fellowship. Whenever missionaries were visiting Basonga, Brabanta Christians came and voiced their complaints.

"Why are we persecuted this way?" they would ask. "For what reason can't we have a place to worship of our own? Suppose we adults do encourage ourselves and keep following Christ; what of our children? In the classroom they are taught to kneel and pray to Mary and the saints. When they grow up, will they follow our footsteps? Why are our missionaries abhorred like lepers and not permitted to stay with us overnight? Is there no way God can open up for us a tiny hole through which we can begin to find a path of our own?"

And missionaries, while hurting with them, could only use again the same worn platitudes to console, explain, encourage, and pray.

Kazadi was ordained to the ministry in 1941 and shortly thereafter accepted the challenge to go with his family to live at Basonga. He would head up the work of this northern region. Some months later Archie received a letter from him.

"The work is growing rapidly," he wrote. "Over a hundred converts wait to be baptized. God is bringing us many new people. Our mud-and-stick chapel is no longer adequate; every Sunday it is packed, and people remain standing outside. People here have heard about what we did to our church at Charlesville. They have chosen a treasurer, and Christians are giving money to a building fund. They are prepared to give themselves to the work. We have no burnt brick or stone here; we will need to build with sun-dried brick. When the season of rain ends so that we can start making bricks, we beg for you and Mutekemena to come sit with us some weeks, to help us build a big house of worship."

Graber was excited at the prospect. Yet he felt some uneasiness about the scope of the undertaking. Just what had Kazadi promised his people? Did he really understand what such an undertaking involved? Would they be able to complete the project in the time allotted, or would Kazadi need to modify his expectations?

One day during early dry season, Archie rented a large truck. He and his workers loaded it with camping equipment, food, tools, and construction materials. The next morning some of his better-trained carpenters and masons mounted themselves on top of the load, he and Evelyn climbed into the cab, and they left. They wended their way for seven hours over 140 miles of hilly dirt roads to Basonga. Graber and his wife set up their temporary home in a grass-roofed, mud-walled hut with an open doorway. After supper that night, the missionary sat with Pastor Kazadi near an outside fire and talked plans.

"Where are you going to get water to make all that sun-dried brick?" Graber asked. "The river is a mile from here."

"I have already arranged for our Christian women to carry it in basins and water gourds on their heads from the river," the black pastor calmly replied. "They'll dump it into two empty gas drums we have here."

"You talk about poles for the roof and lumber for the benches. I wasn't able to bring that much lumber with me. What is your thinking about this?"

"I have a friend who works in the forest as a sawyer. He is loaning us two long lumber saws. I'll send a group of men into the forest tomorrow morning. While we begin digging the foundation here, they can begin cutting poles and lumber."

"We'll need money to buy cement," Graber rejoined. "And the carpenters and masons who have left their homes to come help us, we will need to pay them. Have you got money for these things?"

"Preacher, we've been thinking about all these things for a long time. We've been praying about building our church. Out in all these villages, groups of Christians are praying about it. If the money we have already received is not sufficient, more will come."

Graber blinked, gazing aimlessly into the darkness. In many ways this would be a replay of the 1939 Charlesville church renovation program. But strangely, roles had switched. He, the white man, had uneasiness about the outcome of the project; and Kazadi, brimming with confidence, was firmly in charge. Here the pastor's qualities of leadership would meet their real test.

Graber retired and awoke with daybreak. The sounds of subdued voices and shuffling feet outside caught his attention. He got up off his cot, dressed, and left the hut. A large group of volunteer workers was already gathered. Kazadi sent the women to the river. He divided the men into four groups: the first began digging clay to make brick; the second went to the forest to cut lumber and poles; the third, supervised by the masons, began clearing ground to dig the foundation; carpenters began dressing lumber for church benches.

A daily routine developed which ran with clockwork efficiency. Work began when the stars were still shining and stopped when the first star appeared at night. The number of volunteers coming for work every day never diminished. Morning workmen were joined in midafternoon by men with regular full-time employment who came to help after work hours. The water barrels were never empty. There were no angry reprimands; instead, with good-natured banter, they goaded each other to work. After supper they conducted evangelistic services in nearby villages and took up offerings for the building program.

"We worked that way for six weeks and finished the job," Graber recalled later. "As the work neared its end, they couldn't restrain themselves from singing and rejoicing. They completed debt-free, a beautiful, white twenty-four-by-sixty-foot building with large round pillars, cement floors, and benches, which is still standing today. They had a dedication service with an overflow crowd and about fifteen special numbers; it lasted for three hours, and nobody thought it was too long. That was an outstanding adventure of my missionary career. It showed me what a gifted leader Kazadi was. He knew his Bible. He lived it. People respected him. This experience showed me more than any other what these people are able to do for themselves if they put their hearts into it."

Christians from Brabanta shared in the joy of what happened at Basonga. However, the experience left them more acutely aware of what religious suppression was costing them; it heightened their determination to break free from it. Finally they found that tiny hole they had been praying for, through which they hoped to begin finding a path of their own. Pastor Kazadi reported it to Graber.

"In the matter of both Catholics and Protestants wanting to put teachers in villages," he said, "the government has begun to respect the word of the village chief. If a chief with at least five of his village men goes to the local colonial government man and asks for a certain kind of teacher, his request will be honored."

"Yes, I know that is true," Graber affirmed.

"Do you remember that village just across the plantation boundary line? Its chief is our friend. He and some of his people went to the government man and asked for a teacher from the Protestant mission. He

has given us a parcel of ground on which to build a chapel. The Brabanta
Christians are rejoicing. They see that God is answering their prayers.
The Catholic church has no authority to interfere with their worshiping
in this village. They are waiting for us to come and help them build their
own chapel.''

Archie and Kazadi went to the village, confirmed that the chief had
been granted permission to secure a Protestant teacher, and then
mobilized the Christians to build the chapel. It would be a smaller,
less-impressive structure than the Basonga church. But to the Brabanta
Christians, it would be of far greater significance. It would not only be a
place where they could gather for worship. It would be a symbol that the
iron grip of an irksome religious hierarchy was finally breaking; it would
publicly affirm that they were a people whose conscience should be
respected, and who deserved a place in their own right.

People set to work with a will. Volunteers from the village worked
full-time, and every day at midafternoon employees from the planta-
tions finished their work shift and came to join them. With mounting
excitement they watched the building take shape. They built sun-dried-
brick walls. They erected pole rafters. They tied rattan framework across the rafters. Then the day came when they began tying the
roof covering onto the rattan framework. It was late afternoon. Most of
the workmen were on the roof, unrolling long rolls of sewn palm-leaf
matting and tying it in place. Graber and Kazadi were in conversation
near the church. Suddenly they were interrupted by the sound of an
approaching motorcycle. It brought a white-robed Catholic priest. He
arrived, dismounted, approached the work site, and began ordering
workmen down off the roof.

''What are you doing?'' Graber accosted him.

People from the ends of the village came running to witness the
confrontation. Plantation employees on the roof watched with bated
breath, fearing their long-coveted goal was about to slip from their
grasp.

''Those men are plantation workers,'' the priest replied. ''They
have no right to work for you.''

''Why can't they work for me? They aren't your slaves. They can
do what they want to.''

There followed a prolonged exchange of angry, mounting
polemics. Graber climaxed it by pushing the man toward his cycle.

"Do you want to start a fight?" the priest demanded.

"What did you come here for?" Graber retorted. "You came to start a fight. We aren't bothering you. Get out of here!"

The priest mounted his cycle and left. Workers and village people suddenly found vent for long, pent-up frustration; simultaneously they roared a huzzah after him. Men on the roof were electrified with victory. Their fingers raced at tying the mat to the rattan framework. Someone lifted his voice in a traditional chanting work chorus, and everyone lustily joined him. The song bound them together as one. Kazadi, standing alone, watched with quiet satisfaction for a time. Then a workman heaved a roll of matting onto the roof and came toward him.

"Pastor, Lutonga is calling you."

"Where is he?"

'In that hut over there where we store roof matting."

Kazadi went to the hut and found Archie seated on the piled rolls of palm-leaf matting. His face was drawn with anxiety.

"Father," the pastor asked, "is there something bothering you?"

"Those words I told the priest, do you think they were suitable?"

"Yes, sir. They were good," Kazadi affirmed.

"But all the village people watching and listening . . . what do they think?"

"Don't you hear all those Christians singing out there? Does it appear they think you did something wrong?"

"But you heard the priest's words. He said he would take me to court. Don't you think I should go arrange things with him?"

"For what reason? After what has happened, you want to go make confession to him? Why should you repent to him? What you did gave us courage. Don't you hear our joy? Now you want to ruin everything by going to him to say that you were wrong. After you do that and return, then what will you say to us? You haven't broken any laws of the government. You've done nothing wrong that needs to be fixed up."

"We could see plainly the kind of heart this white man had," Kazadi explained later. "When someone wanted to obstruct what Lutonga believed was the will of God, he had quick anger. But he never held contempt for anyone. He never carried ill will in his heart. He was angry with the person's wrong deeds. More than anything else, he wanted to be the friend of everybody. I can't count the times we fussed at each other. But our arguings helped bond us together until we were like the sons of one father.''

Gradually, over succeeding years, the prayers of Brabanta's believers were answered; they found freedom of religion and had classes for their children. Graber and Kazadi recognized that such mutual experiences revealed qualities in each of them which the other esteemed. This growing appreciation for each other strengthened bonds between them. But neither of them guessed that the day was coming when these bonds would be put to the severest test.

12

... Closing an Era ...

EVELYN'S FAILING HEALTH took the Grabers home to the States in August 1946. Over the succeeding months, in spite of their best efforts, her situation did not improve. In June 1947, their doctor recommended total rest. Archie purchased a house trailer, parked it in a vacant country schoolyard a few miles south of Bloomington, Illinois, near friends and medical help, and took care of her. In May 1948, when Archie was on board the S.S. *Lindi* headed for Africa, he wrote a letter which will complete the story.

"One morning a few brief months ago, when we were living in our house trailer, I was feeling very depressed. It seemed to me I could see that great door to Africa slowly closing me off from people there who are as dear to me as life itself. I asked God for courage, and a promise from His holy Word was given me: 'Behold, I am with thee, and will keep thee in all places whither thou goest, and will bring thee again into this land; for I will not leave thee, until I have done that which I have spoken to thee of' (Gen. 28:15).

"The next day we went to see the doctor. After receiving this promise from the Lord, I thought we would hear good news. But it was not as we expected. Instead, he said he could do no more for my wife, and asked us to try Chicago, or Rochester, Minnesota. We decided to go to Chicago. After ten days of examinations, one of the specialists called me out of my wife's room. He told me that she could not get well, and that she would have less than three months to live. I left the hospital and went to my room in the YMCA. Again I cried to God for grace and strength and courage. The same verse came to me again; but this time I read it differently than when I had read it in the schoolyard. The first time I thought it meant that both of us would return to Congo, but now I came to understand that I would go alone, and the living Christ who had gone with us together before, was now going with me.[1]

"Her presence in the schoolroom and church will be greatly missed; her sweet singing around the campfires and in our home is now stilled. Yet we know God makes no mistakes. He is working out His purpose. He does not ask us to understand it all now. So until the mist has rolled away, I feel I can pay no greater tribute to her than to carry on the great work which was so dear to her heart, and is to mine."[2]

Archie was asked to carry on that work by attempting to establish a new mission station a hundred miles south of Charlesville, at Tshikapa. The town's native population approximated fifteen thousand. It was an industrial center for diamond mining. The company was owned, controlled, and operated by Belgians; and the spiritual interests of its workmen were even more jealously guarded by a Catholic hierarchy than had been the case on the Brabanta oil plantation.

Graber arrived on the field and contemplated his next step. Many good things had happened at Charlesville during the seventeen years he and Evelyn had lived there, and he was grateful. The station, which in 1930 had consisted of four brick missionary dwellings and a church, now boasted an impressive complex of buildings: the press-and-office structure, an eight-unit primary school, a teacher-training school, dormitory buildings, a maternity hospital, and a fifth dwelling. Missionary personnel had grown from five to nine.

Likewise the church had progressed. Old Djoko Punda, the chief who originally gave the land on which the station was built, was one among many in the immediate area who had surrendered to Christ. Baptized Christians in the total geographic region for which Charlesville Station was responsible now numbered over 5,000; villages where resident mission teachers shepherded flocks of believers approached 100. To the far north, in the Basonga-Brabanta region, Pastor Kazadi and a complement of strong leaders were in charge of a growing work. Plans were in the offing for a senior missionary couple to establish a station among the Bashilele, a head-hunting tribe long the concern of Graber, which occupied most of the region west of Charlesville. Average attendance at Sunday morning worship service on the station was

[1]Date of decease: November 3, 1947
[2]*Congo Missionary Messenger,* July-August 1948, p. 16.

668. Archie recalled his first trip south in 1932 through the heavily populated Tshikapa area; what he saw then prompted him to hope for the day when the Protestant mission could plant a permanent witness there. His beloved wife, whose life was so inextricably interwoven with all that had happened at Charlesville, was now gone. This door to a new work had opened, making his long-held hope a possibility. He was ready to go.

Graber loaded his camping equipment into a new gray Ford pickup he had brought with him to the field and went to a large village near Tshikapa to see his old friend Chief Kalonda. The chief assigned Lutonga living quarters in his compound . . . a grass-roofed mud hut large enough for his camp cot and, next to it, a kitchen shack. Here Archie lived, visiting with the population, initiating friendships with Belgian diamond mine authorities, and nudging colonial government officials to grant him a plot of ground. In spite of incredible odds, at the end of eighteen months he was given twenty acreas of land on a neglected hillside overlooking the Kasai River three miles from the center of town. Thus he was officially authorized to establish himself at Tshikapa. Graber thanked Chief Kalonda for his hospitality and went to Charlesville to get his things.

It was April 1950. The program on Charlesville station had long been adjusted to allow for Graber's departure. It remained for him to take care of a few final business matters, say good-by to his friends, pack and load his personal effects, and leave. During those few days everything went according to plan until the pickup, backed to his doorstep, was almost loaded and he was on the point of departure. He noticed Mbuyi and his five-year-old daughter standing forlornly to one side, their faces the picture of bereavement. Archie let others bring the last articles from the house and went to speak to Mbuyi.

"Father Mbuyi, do you have a word with me?" Graber looked down at the wrinkled little man.

"My preacher, all these many years I've lived close to you. I've worked hard for you. Of all the things you ever asked me to do, I never refused once. Now why are you saying today that you are abandoning me — I cannot go with you?"

"I haven't forgotten you," Lutonga replied. "I discussed the matter with the church council. To begin a new station, one must suffer. At the place I am going to, there is nothing. I will build a house of mud and sticks and sit there alone, in the high grass. A place like that is not good for two small children. Here your children can go to school. If sickness catches them, there is medicine. The church council decided that it would be better for you to stay.''

''All these years you've been telling us to put our faith in God. You sat there for eighteen months. You have been telling us of all the miracles that God did for you there. The God who has been taking care of you there, isn't He able to take care of us?''

''But you know that you are having trouble with chest sickness,'' Archie rejoined. ''From time to time you need medicine for it. The missionary nurse says you should stay here for treatment. At Tshikapa sitting in the high grass on that empty hillside, where would you get medicine? Your sickness will grow. You'll suffer helplessly and die.''

''Preacher, it is already written that I will die. If you make me sit here alone to die, do you think that will be a death of happiness? Let us go sit at the same place with you. Then I will die with happiness.''

''But my friend,'' Lutonga argued, ''those two girls need a father. You are no longer a young man. For many years you made foot trips to carry the mission mailbag. This work has left your body weak. You should take good care of your body so that you can be with your daughters until they are grown.''

''You say my body is old and weak?''

The little man turned heel and took off down the road running at full speed, his calloused feet kicking up tufts of sand, until he disappeared over the hill two hundred yards away. In a few moments he appeared again, running the full distance back without slacking his pace.

''Did you see that?'' he asked, catching his breath. ''You say I'm an old sick man with a weak body. Tell me truthfully, preacher, why are you abandoning us today?''

''What else can I say?'' Lutonga shrugged. ''Go get your things and put them onto the truck.''

While Graber finished moving out of the house, Mbuyi loaded his few pieces of furniture. Delela stacked their belongings onto two spread-out blankets, folded up their corners and tied them to make compact bundles, and hoisted them up to loaders on the back of the truck. When the loading was finished, Delela and the younger girl got into the cab beside Graber; Mbuyi and the older girl sat themselves on top of the load in back; and they left. They were happy to wave good-by. They were looking forward to clearing grass and bush on an isolated hillside a hundred miles away and starting a new home.

These events were shaping Lutonga. They would one day help him provide Kazadi with the answer to his question about how the tragic brokenness of his people could ever be healed.

Part 2

... A Drying Stalk ...

13

... 1950–1959:

Economic Transition ...

FEW PEOPLE NOTICED it, but at the point where Graber left his Charlesville friends, Africa was beginning to feel the birth-pangs of freedom. The process of bringing the people of Africa to birth in freedom would not be easy. Labor would be a quarter of a century long; its convulsive agonies would rack the entire continent. Nowhere were labor pains more excruciating than in Congo. They led its unsuspecting people into an era of unprecedented crisis. And at the point where crisis peaked, Graber would meet his Charlesville friends again.

From the fifteenth century, by means of arbitrary claims and military conquest, the white man came to rule almost all of black Africa. His power was generally undisputed until after World War II, when the heady breezes of political independence began wafting across the continent. Some colonial powers began to bend their policies with the growing winds of nationalism. In 1946 France granted its African colonies considerable power over their affairs; in 1958 French President De Gaulle offered political independence to any territory requesting it. Britain granted independence to Sudan in 1956, to Ghana in 1957, and scheduled the soon transfer of power in the rest of her African colonies.

In contrast, Belgium decided to stone-wall the winds of change. She would divert the attention of her black subjects from nationalistic aspirations by lavishing upon them a cornucopia of social benefits, and would vigorously suppress any who could not thereby be pacified. "Dominate in order to serve" was her plan.[1] One Belgian described the

[1]The title of a book (*Dominer Pour Servir*) by Pierre Ryckmans, a former governor general to the colony, which described the philosophy of the Belgian administration.

policy in more mundane terms, as that of a parent who says to his children at the table, "Don't talk with your mouths full." [2]

Pursuing such a policy was clearly a gamble, and Belgium staked what eventually came to be an investment of $8 billion on its success.[3] The policy was promoted by a white-power league of government, big business, and the Roman Catholic Church. It was enforced by a well-disciplined army of 25,000 blacks under the command of 1000 Belgian officers.

Social development of the colony was structured into a $960 million Ten-Year Plan, which covered the period 1950–1959. The Belgian government utilized expanding revenue from the colony's fabulous resources to help pay for it. By 1958 Congo was the world's leading producer of uranium, cobalt, cadmium, and industrial diamonds; mines at Tshikapa alone produced over half a million carats of diamonds a year. These commodities plus copper, zinc, manganese, rubber, cotton, and palm oil earned Belgium $200 million a year, and produced revenue to fund 70 percent of the Ten-Year Plan.

This kind of response to events on the continent produced an era of rapid economic transition in Congo. The father worked hard to fill the children's mouths and hoped they would settle into peaceful slumber. Expanding business and industry brought increased employment. Workers across the colony were guaranteed a minimum wage, housing, free medical service, and pension benefits. Trading posts scattered along 70,000 miles of maintained dirt roads provided points where rural population could sell produce from their fields and purchase merchandise, its variety ever expanding, abreast with growing national affluence.

By 1958, 2,468 hospitals brought medical treatment to the majority of the colony's population of twelve million. Diseases such as small pox and sleeping sickness were all but stamped out. Infant mortality in some areas was reduced to a rate lower than that of some European countries. The portion of Congo's school-age children in school climbed to 50 percent, the highest average for any country in Africa.

The impact of these events was far-reaching. From time immemorial, native Congolese had lived in the cruel clutches of poverty. From generation to generation, people had been destined to lives of grinding

---

[2]"After 50 Years," *Time,* October 27, 1958, p. 29.
[3]"For Belgium: $8 Billion at Stake," *U.S. News & World Report,* August 1, 1960.

toil to fend off death by starvation, exposure, or disease. Now the Ten-Year Plan for social development was changing all that. A few tribespeople responded with apathy; they were too thoroughly steeped in tradition, or their incentive for self-improvement had been all but snuffed out. But most Congolese, and particularly those from more progressive tribes, recognized that social development now being fostered by the colonial government provided for them an opportunity to finally break free from the clutches of poverty; and they seized it with enthusiasm.

Such was the case with Pastor Kazadi. He had long recognized that people living on the bedrock of poverty had no means for supporting an autonomous native church; he wanted to inspire people to reach for a higher standard of living. He wanted to prove to fellow church leaders that they didn't need to live as second-class citizens on the meager offerings of their church people; by hard work it was now possible for them to improve their lots. He wanted to secure for himself and his family a stronger financial base.

In 1950 Kazadi transferred the responsibility of the work at Basonga to an ordained pastor and a team of leaders whom he had trained and returned to Charlesville. He located at Kahemba, an outpost south across the river from the mission station and six miles east, along a main road. He borrowed money and hired workmen to help him clear tracts of land for cornfields and a coffee plantation, and he pastored the small local church.

By 1959 Congolese in general, and at Charlesville in particular, had come to enjoy a standard of living which could hardly have been imagined when Graber first arrived in 1930. Cast-off American garments, which were then prestige symbols, were now considered suitable only for work. Now on Sunday at church, children wore neat, ready-made clothing freshly laundered; the mother wore a tailor-made blouse and skirt of brightly designed cloth, a colorful head bandanna, and patent leather sandals; the father wore a white shirt, a necktie, tailor-made trousers freshly pressed with a charcoal iron, and polished shoes.

Most families had graduated from one-room huts to two- or three-room homes. Some homes were constructed of sun-dried brick; occasionally they were roofed with corrugated sheet metal. The father no longer slept on a hard bamboo rack; the mother no longer slept on a mat on the floor. They slept in a bedroom, on a wooden bedframe supporting a thick straw tick, or in occasional cases, an innerspring mattress. The sitting room was furnished with a few wooden armchairs with loose cushions, arranged around a small center table, which often held a bouquet of artificial flowers. In the center of the dining room was a square table with a few straight-backed chairs; along a side wall was a small buffet with window-glass doors displaying an arduously collected variety of table dishes and stainless steel eating utensils.

Diets now utilized a larger variety of food items, including canned meats purchased at local trading centers. Breakfast was coming into vogue. For children this could mean cooked oatmeal or cornmeal mush; for adults it meant generously sweetened tea heavily diluted with powdered milk, fresh bread from a nearby home bakery, and fruit in season.

Virtually every household had at least one bicycle; a few had motorbikes. A person of extremely good fortune might have occasion to travel overseas; he would bring back with him extraordinary symbols of Western affluence. In 1957 Pastor Kazadi was brought to North America to visit churches supporting mission work in his country. American friends helped him secure a twelve-gauge shotgun to provide more meat for his family's diet and a washing machine powered by a gasoline motor. People emerging from long poverty relished such material benefits and hoped they would last forever.

The rapid social development of this era was a contributing factor to the rapid growth of the mission work. From the beginning of 1950 to the end of 1959, the Africa Inter-Mennonite Mission (then known as the Congo Inland Mission) doubled the number of its mission stations from four to eight. The number of baptized Christians in its assigned area grew from 8,765 to 22,876; their annual per capita giving trebled; and the number of national pastors shepherding them grew from nine to 27. Kazadi was elected president of this emerging national church. At his post at Kahemba, an attractive stone edifice and parsonage were built, and attendance at Sunday worship service averaged 200.

One of these stations opened on the field of the AIMM was the center of Graber's new work near Tshikapa. He named it "Kalonda," after the chief who had provided him with a place to live during his first eighteen months there. In April 1951, Archie Graber married Irma Beitler, a missionary nurse serving at Charlesville. Early the following year, Nancy, their first child, was born.

Archie never regretted that Mbuyi and Delela had come with him.

During the early months, hours with them around the bonfire at night helped alleviate the loneliness. In 1956 Mbuyi was cited by the colonial government for thirty years of service to the colony. He continued unswervingly loyal to his death in 1958.

Impetus from the colony's social progress was felt in the work at Kalonda also. By the time the Grabers went on furlough in mid-1959, Archie had constructed, with baked brick, four missionary dwellings, an eight-room primary school building, a medical dispensary, a Bible institute building, and an impressive church. The station was staffed by seven missionaries. Its work had won the respect of diamond mine authorities, a permanent church had been constructed in the mining company's principal work camp in the city of Tshikapa, and a national pastor was living in its parsonage.

And so, across the colony, Belgium aggressively pursued her ten-year gamble. For more than half of those years, it looked as if she just might win. The father worked indefatigably to keep the mouths full. But his children would not thereby be lulled to sleep. Many of them continued enjoying the meal. But a few, whose minds were forming unconventional questions about the family's future, began rustling their feet annoyingly beneath the table and would not be stopped.

In early 1958 Pastor Kazadi toured AIMM stations to report to Congolese audiences on his trip to North America. A recurring incident illustrates the separation of those who were beginning to rustle their feet from those who were content to keep on eating.

Educated young men were beginning to scrutinize the Africans' long-ingrained feeling that only white man's culture was good, while their own was largely worthless. They asked questions that openly challenged the white man's presumed infallibility.

"Did you see any drunk people in America?" they would ask.

Kazadi was not easily disconcerted.

"I may have seen someone drunk," he replied, "but I did not stop and write it down in my notebook. When I was in America, suppose I would have made it my primary task to make a record of every drunk person I saw; then I would have returned to our country and showed you the list. Would you say that my trip to America had been worthwhile? Would this news be of value to you? I went to America to learn things that will help us. One important lesson I learned is that Americans don't pick money off of trees. They don't sit looking at the sun. They work day and night. Everybody works.''

So Kazadi, fusing this lesson to the economic opportunities of the moment, returned to his coffee plantation and worked. Meanwhile, younger men kept raising their questions.

In keeping with its colonial policy, the Belgian government discouraged higher education for blacks. It trained a professional cadre only large enough to pursue its long-range interests in the colony. But such a policy was on collision course with the growing determination of awakening Africans to be in charge of their own destinies and to earn a place in the world in their own right. The availability of transistor radios and the availability of secondary education — though limited — were both benefits deriving from the Ten-Year Plan. The first brought them regular news of rising political expectations elsewhere in Africa, and the second made them cognizant of the fact that they themselves were coming of age. For growing numbers, the father's food lost its flavor. Children emptied their mouths, announced their expectations, and eventually began pounding the table insisting that the father get out of the house. They would rather prepare their own meals and eat poorly than have him feed them any longer.

14

... 1955–1959:
Political Transition ...

IN DECEMBER OF 1955, A. A. J. Van Bilsen, a Belgian professor, published a paper in which he declared that self-determination for the Congo was inevitable, and proposed a 30-year plan toward the eventual transfer of power.[1] Response to the paper portended the future. Most Belgians considered it dangerously radical. On the other hand, leaders of ABAKO, a native cultural society in Leopoldville, said that thirty years was much too long; they insisted that preparations begin at once.[2] With this event, the long-confined genie escaped from the bottle and would never go back in again.

For taking such a view, ABAKO leaders were imprisoned. In counter-response, the organization shifted its interests from culture to politics and promoted the cause of self-government. In August 1956, black nationalists clearly stated their demands in a manifesto published in a small newspaper, *Conscience Africaine*. Reaction of the masses in the capital city to the declaration was described as "electric." Over ensuing months, leaders from an increasing number of predominant tribes formed political parties and joined the cause. In December 1958, leaders from the two principal parties attended a Pan-African Congress in Ghana and were greeted as champions for the cause of African nationalism.

[1]"Un Plan de Trente Ans Pour l'Emancipation Politique de l'Afrique Belge," by A. A. J. Van Bilsen.
[2]Cultural society of the Bakongo peoples, descendants of an ancient powerful west coast tribal kingdom.

Response of the Belgian government of these developments indicated that it did not recognize how powerfully the genie was working its magic. A colonial minister who favored emancipation was replaced by an arch-conservative. Plans to increase the pace of leadership training were stymied. Efforts to hold nationalistic enthusiasm in check were made with a big stick of selected arrests in one hand and the carrot of arrangements for low-level elections in the other.

But aspirations for self-rule were too powerful to contain. Eventually they exploded in the Leopoldville riots of January 1959. An estimated three hundred Congolese were reported killed or wounded. This event shook the Belgian administration from its lethargy, compelled it to draw up for its colony a new structure of government that allowed growing participation of blacks, and announced to the world that political independence for Congo was no longer an option.

Tribal leaders across the country were now compelled to anticipate what their role would be in an independent Congo. They formed political parties to lay claim to their share of self-rule. Such tribally oriented parties proliferated to a total of two hundred; party spokesmen established their respective positions along the spectrum of nationalistic demands, from radical to conciliatory, and drew lines of battle with competing politicians.

Nowhere were these lines more sharply drawn than between the Baluba and the Lulua. The Baluba, because of their aggressiveness and application, had come to fill most key positions in commerce, industry, and government in the traditional Lulua area. They saw this as the moment to exploit their advantage, and so made aggressive demands for immediate independence.

The native Lulua, who numbered about 450,000, insisted that immediate independence would be catastrophic. It was intolerable to think that people who had served them as slaves two generations earlier should now rule them. They were basically committed to the Belgian government's plan for a gradual transfer to self-government. And they hoped that in the interim, their people could be trained for key positions to replace the Baluba. "If you want independence," they told the Baluba, "go back to South Kasai, where you came from, and run your government as you like."

The Baluba were not ready to sacrifice their homes and jobs to conciliate a tribe that had once enslaved them. "We know why you want to stall off political independence'' was their reply. ''But we've worked hard to get where we are. And we're staying here. We once took orders from the Lulua, but never again.''

The power struggle centered 155 miles east of Charlesville, in Luluabourg, capital of Kasai Province, a city of 80,000 in the heart of Lulua country. Kalamba Mangole, chief of the Lulua, watched these trends with consternation. Tensions between people of the two tribes living in the city mounted. Progress toward black rule was unrelenting. In May 1959 he demanded that the Belgian colonial administration recognize the existence of a Lulua kingdom as an identified entity. It appeared he hoped to use such recognition as legal sanction to force the Baluba to leave. His demand was rejected.

The Lulua accused the Baluba of paying the Belgian head of the provincial government 500 million francs and a box of diamonds to keep their positions of power. The Baluba said that Lulua Chief Kalamba had called together two hundred subchiefs. These chiefs killed and ate a cow, covenanting that they would not meet again and share a second cow until the Baluba had been expelled. During September rumors persisted of an ''arms race''; arrows, spears, and swords were being gathered for inevitable war.

At this point Albert Kalonji, a Baluba political leader who was to play a key role in the desperate days ahead, accused the colonial government of deliberately fomenting discord between his people and the Lulua. When he and two colleagues were arrested, the Baluba rioted.

In Luluabourg, fighting between the two tribes broke out on October 13, 1959, and triggered sporadic warfare which stretched into the succeeding months. It sped along the roads reaching out from the city, like fire following the fuse-spokes of a wheel. Every fresh outbreak spawned an ensuing one. The strife left in its wake burned-out homes and dead bodies ghastly mutilated. Ahead of it, hordes of terror-stricken Baluba refugees fled across the eastern border of Lulua land, to their ancestral homeland in South Kasai.

Civil disorders were not confined to the Lulua–Baluba area. On October 14 rioting broke out in the port city of Matadi on the west coast; twenty-eight persons were hospitalized. Patrice Lumumba had emerged as the colony's most aggressive spokesman for nationalism. On October 30 he spoke at a mass rally at the northeastern city of Stanleyville. His supporters rioted, and security forces intervened; twenty-six were killed and over a hundred wounded. Less-publicized incidents of violence became increasingly frequent, and Belgian-commanded military units made desperate efforts to stitch together a rapidly fragmenting society.

If such signs portended ill for the future, black nationalists gave them no heed. On the contrary, politicians relentlessly urged the Belgian administration to hasten the transfer of power. Finally, the government in Brussels called a Round Table Conference for January 20, 1960, and invited ninety-six Congolese leaders to participate. Their average age was thirty-five, their average education less than high school. At this conference, the date for political independence was set for June 30, 1960.

Congolese in the colony's less-populated rural areas could not remain unaffected by these events. When the winds of nationalism began stirring, people of Charlesville and its environs tried to understand the implications of self-rule in their respective tribal contexts. This led to surmising the intentions of tribes adjacent to them, which spawned suspicions, then accusations, then threats and counter-threats of violence. In this process, every person was compelled to choose between powerfully competing loyalties.

Church leaders living in the Christian village adjacent to the mission compound withstood formidable pressures from their respective tribal peers and affirmed their common loyalty to the tribe of Jesus Christ. "Politicians are lusting for power," they would say. "Earthly chiefs are trying to carve out their separate kingdoms. Greed is stirring up all this fighting. Satan wants to use it to chop the church into little pieces. We belong to Chief Jesus; our kingdom is in heaven." They worked hard to rally Christians behind them.

Baluba tribesmen lived in the rows of homes closest to the mission station; and beyond them, row after row, extended the homes of Lulua. At first the two groups summarily refused to allow tribal tensions to affect them. They had lived together in peace for years. Their yards were linked with well-worn paths of friendship. Many from the two tribes had intermarried. Then the winds of news and rumor began to rise . . . winds that mounted in force to pummel them incessantly and mercilessly.

A daughter on a journey was caught in warfare and had disappeared. A pregnant niece was shot down when fleeing from her hut, set on fire by night marauders. Long-established Baluba village chiefs began moving their people out of the Lulua area. Students returned home from distant schools closed by tribal strife. An aunt was kidnapped by attacking warriors. The body of an uncle was found along a roadside, his hands and testicles severed. A fresh outbreak of war along a main road brought strife a few miles closer.

"Can we renounce the bonds of human kinship?" people asked. "When a relative is lost or slain, do we not mourn? And how do our hearts feel toward relatives of his assailants who live near us? What wisdom shall we follow when this fighting reaches us?" So news spread. Rumors flowed. Fears grew. Tensions climbed. Church leaders and missionaries worked tirelessly to keep people calm.

The hill slope directly across the river from the mission station was covered with huts of a large Lulua residential quarter. One night in early January 1960, Baluba men, armed with European shotguns and riding in an automobile, launched an attack on Lulua residing there. Rev. and Mrs. Glenn Rocke lived on the mission station, in the house long occupied by Archie Graber. Mrs. Rocke would never forget that night.

"Glenn was gone on a trip to take the children back to boarding school," she recalled. "That evening our dog began howling uncontrollably. I couldn't figure out what was the matter. Then about ten o'clock, we heard shooting and saw huts burning across the river. The noises were awful."

On the morning following the attack, a missionary took the ferry across the river to do evangelistic work in the villages. He found the Lulua city deserted. About two hundred houses were burned. Eight persons were slain; fourteen lay wounded, abandoned when panicking villagers took flight. He loaded his vehicle with wounded and returned to the mission station. Of the fourteen brought to the hospital, four died from excessive blood loss during the night, or from extensive wounds.

"When people saw the wounded arrive from across the river," Mrs. Rocke said, "news spread like wildfire to the Christian village. People began flocking down from the village onto the mission station. They were out of their minds with fear. They swarmed into the medical buildings and into our homes for refuge. They packed themselves under tables and inside of closets. There must have been almost a hundred in our house . . . people of both tribes. Then men armed with knives, arrows, and spears closed the doors, and lay down on the floor across them. Refugees stayed in the house that way the rest of the day, and all night, and finally began dispersing the following morning. Some of them kept coming back night after night for about a week.''

A rapid succession of events continued to pummel emotions. The rumor spread that the carload of Baluba men was preparing to cross to the mission side of the river to launch a night attack on the Lulua portion of the Christian village. Lulua men across the river, bent on revenging the initial attack, beat out war messages on drums calling for the support of fellow Lulua at the mission. A Belgian-commanded military force intercepted a large group of armed Lulua warriors moving toward Charlesville to launch a retaliatory attack on the Baluba; it opened fire on them, killed some, and wounded others. Someone shot an arrow from ambush at a passing mission vehicle and wounded a missionary in the arm. Missionaries, black church leaders, and the ruling chief of each of the rival tribes in the Christian village pitted their combined efforts against the mounting tensions for war and were able to enforce an uneasy peace.

The black leader who might have been most influential in keeping peace was Pastor Kazadi. Over the years, his incisiveness and impartiality had earned him the highest respect of all tribal groups represented in the church. But in the maelstrom of preindependence events, respect for him eroded, and consequently, his power to negotiate intertribal disputes waned.

''Why do people no longer respect the word of Pastor Kazadi as they once did?'' missionaries would ask. Members of the church council put together for them the following explanation:

''Baluba people sitting in villages around Kazadi's outpost at Kahemba said Lulua tribesmen were making medicine to kill them, or were plotting war against them; so they began leaving for the land of their tribal ancestors in South Kasai. The local black government administrator is Lulua; he urged his own tribespeople to occupy the villages vacated by the Baluba.

''When Kazadi saw this, he became concerned. He had his coffee plantation, his large truck, his coffee-hulling machine. He had invested everything in this project. He did not want to lose all these things. He nurtured friendship with Congolese whom Belgians were training for places of leadership in the local government; most of these new leaders were Baluba. They would help Kazadi protect his property.

"People interpret this through the eyes of tribalism. They see that Kazadi had clearly sided with the Baluba against the Lulua. For a long time some people have been jealous of his financial prosperity. Now when they see he has taken sides, they accuse him vehemently. They say that his American gun was seen in the hands of Baluba attackers the night the city was burned.

"They say that he is using his contacts with the Belgian and Baluba government agents to get guns and ammunition; he wants to make war to depose the Lulua administrator and replace him with one from the Baluba. When people's hearts are aflame, one can never find the path of truth in such matters. After the Baluba attack, the Belgian government man went to see Kazadi to inspect the gun. Afterwards he told people that the gun had not been used; but people with bad hearts toward Kazadi do not believe his words. Because of all this, people no longer respect the words of Kazadi as they once did."

The last person Congolese would accuse of tribal partiality was the missionary. He was an expatriate; he had brought them the message that God loves everyone equally. And so, increasingly, leaders of rival tribes relied on the missionary to mediate between them to keep the peace. At Charlesville station, missionary Harold Graber served as "chairman" and was titular head of that station's program. Harold (no relation to Archie, and about twenty-five years his junior) was pressed into the role of final arbiter to maintain peace between the Baluba and Lulua living in the Christian village.

Frequently a runner would come in the middle of the night, stand outside Harold's bedroom window, and call him.

"Preacher, come to the village quickly! Agitators from outside are stirring up the Lulua; their criers are calling for war."

"Preacher, warriors from other tribes have joined with the Baluba; they're going to attack us tonight."

Harold would dress, check out the rumor, and then visit the Baluba and Luala chiefs, enlisting their help to quiet their people.

"When you come at night," the two chiefs soon counseled him, "come with a pastor from the accusing tribe to hear everything we say. Otherwise people from that tribe will say that you came so that we could secretly plot against them."

Repeatedly these night treks proved crucial in forestalling violence. Over succeeding months, by means of endless hours of negotiating, leaders were able to hold a shaky peace. Nightly treks became more frequent until they were routine. With each succeeding night, Harold began to discern a growing number of men milling in the streets.

Subsequent events fed the turmoil. Warriors set up roadblocks on tribal borders and harassed passersby. The Lulua purportedly laid an ambush to kill Pastor Kazadi on his return from a conference. A large village was burned to the east of Charlesville. Several were killed in war to the south. Tribal fighting broke out near Charlesville. Mutilated yet living victims were brought to the mission station hospital that day; when people saw them, passions were incited to rage. That night Harold was called to the village.

He found armed men in the streets, waiting for a first incident to trigger violence. Rumors rampaged out of control. Mutual trust was frayed to a few taut strands. Tension was a living, creeping thing that chilled his spine. As he moved along the sandy streets separating the rows of homes, warriors of both sides gave him the same somber prediction.

"Preacher, there is no way of restraining ourselves any longer. The only way we can finish this business is to fight."

It was Saturday, May 28, 1960 . . . one month before the celebration of political independence.

15

... On the Brink of Calamity ...

MIRACULOUSLY, EFFORTS of reconcilers prevailed through the dark threatening hours of that night, and dawn broke peacefully. As on any Lord's Day, the church bell rang, calling people to worship. Missionaries went to church. Harold Graber arrived with his wife and children. He noticed that only a handful of blacks had come . . . Baluba people whose homes were along streets close to the mission compound. Apparently tension in the village was still high; Lulua Christians were afraid to traverse the Baluba residential area to come to church. He and his family took their places in a pew and began to share in the worship service.

There was a tap on his shoulder. It was a Lulua messenger. His face was tense, his eyes large with fright. Harold went with him outside.

"Preacher, the Baluba are lusting for war. They want to drive us out today. The Creator showed me mercy; He helped me steal through Baluba lines to get here. Pastor Kuamba sent me. He wants you to come right away. He begs you to bring other missionary men with you."

Harold called Dr. John Zook and Glenn Rocke from the church service. The messenger set the pace ahead of them. As they strode up the gentle slope toward the village, Harold's thoughts centered on Kuamba. He was a young Lulua pastor . . . a man of small stature and quiet demeanor. His faith and composure had emerged as powerful factors in helping mediate between the tribes. He brought unusual experience to the task.

For eight years he had cared for his invalid wife. She had never borne him a child. She had brought him little remuneration from her work in their fields, as wives were expected to do. For the last three years of her life she was bedfast. In spite of pressure from tribemates to abandon her . . . in spite of personal ridicule and public gossip, he served her in the deepest Christian meaning of the word, to her death.

Now Kuamba exhibited the wages of that service . . . from some deep inner resource he drew patience and strength which seemed indomitable. During these days, the attention of everyone was focused on the one crucial issue of survival. Issues of daily human existence, which on another day had seemed so important, were now trivial; and in the thinking of Baluba and Lulua alike, no black leader was more worthy of their respect and trust than was Pastor Kuamba.

The group of men turned left on one of the first streets of the Christian village, leaving the bulk of the Baluba section to their right. Kuamba, though Lulua, lived in the Baluba area. He had a small cement-block house on the far end of an adjacent street, which he had bought from Baluba in more peaceful days. The part of the village through which they now passed seemed deserted. Those men who had not gone to church apparently had assembled closer to the line of tribal confrontation. The morning silence was broken only by the sounds of their walking and occasional muffled shouting from a distance up the gradual slope to their right.

Pastor Kuamba stood waiting for the missionaries on his open corner veranda. He took them inside. His voice was quiet and controlled.

"Matters have become very difficult now," he said. "Do you hear that noise up there on the hill? Warriors of the two sides are standing in lines facing each other. They are shouting insults at each other. They are trying to ignite the fire of war. The time has arrived for us to show our courage. Let's go walk between the lines to restrain them. We want to speak words that will cool their anger. We need to bring their minds back into paths of reason, so that they will sit down and talk."

The men had a circle of prayer, committing themselves into the hands of God. They left the house and started up the grade into the residential area. They were empty-handed, except for Kuamba, who carried his Bible. They reached the line of confrontation. The scene was frightening.

Baluba warriors stood in a line along the last street of the Baluba section. Lulua warriors stood facing them in a line along the first street of the Lulua section. Only the two rows of thatch-roofed homes which fronted on the parallel streets separated them. The combatants were prepared for battle. Their bodies were whitewashed. Some had painted their faces with slashes of whitewash to look more fierce. From their necks hung small packages of ancestral medicine with supposed power to protect their bodies from harm. In their hands they held bows, arrows, guns, metal-pointed spears, and crude lances made by sharpening the large ends of palm-frond ribs.

They were gripped in a mounting frenzy for war. Brandishing their weapons, they hurled insults at the opposite line.

"You act like a bunch of weak women playing a dancing game. If you want so much to fight, come on and fight."

"Let one of you shoot an arrow, and we'll see who are weak as women. We'll show you the fighting of he-men."

The four men passed the Baluba warriors and walked out between the lines. Response was instantaneous.

"What are you preachers doing here? Step to one side."

"Get out. Stop getting yourselves mixed up in our affairs. We're having it out today."

John began talking to Baluba warriors. Harold walked across to the Lulua lines. The primary aim was to divert the attention of antagonists away from their efforts to inflame each other.

"We do not desire to interfere in your affairs," Harold explained. "Our desire is to save your lives and property. First, put down your weapons. The moment a drop of human blood is shed, what will happen? People created by a God of love do not resolve their problems by butchering each other. They solve their problems by using their minds. When we see blood, we can't think any more. You say the medicine around your necks will protect you? What about warriors who lie in the mission hospital here. They were all cut up in fighting. Why didn't their medicine protect them? If people out in the hill villages want to fight, that is their business. But we are people of God. This is ground of the mission station. It belongs to God. It is hallowed ground. Human blood will not be shed here. Not a single drop."

John gave the same message to the Baluba.

Harold paused a moment to look around him. Where were all the other Congolese church leaders? They'd always stood with him before. Apparently this time tension ran so high that none of them felt safe to expose himself. There in an open yard between two homes in no man's land, Kuamba with his Bible stood alone. His voice was raised in entreaty.

"My friends . . . my kinsmen. Why are you rushing into the direction of fighting rapidly like this? Take your thinking out of the path of war. Don't you fear the warnings of our ancestors about shedding human blood? Fighting will destroy everything. It will divide us perpetually. We are Christians. There is another way to resolve our differences."

Rocke was talking with the Lulua warriors; he was holding their attention. Harold went to see the Lulua chief at his home nearby.

"Chief," he said, "your warriors are terribly upset. They have reason to be upset. Things have happened which make them very angry. The same is true of the Baluba warriors. But these things can never be resolved by killing one another. The only way people can be reconciled is by talking together. Why don't you chiefs each bring three of your warriors so that we can meet together to talk? Maybe we can curb this passion for fighting and restore peace."

"If the Baluba chief agrees to your plan," the chief responded, "we will pursue it."

The Baluba chief supported the plan.

The chiefs went to their respective lines and announced their decision. Some warriors protested vehemently. Others reluctantly agreed and proceeded to select their representatives. Slowly, conferees responded. They gave their weapons to others, moved onto neutral ground between the lines, cautiously approached each other, and began consultation. A few combatants, still determined to fight, persisted in shouting insults. Chiefs ordered them to keep quiet and to hold their positions. Negotiations continued for about an hour. Tension between the participants subsided to the point where the church leaders and chiefs won the support of the warrior delegations to abandon plans for confrontation and to work for reconciliation. They had prayer together. Then tribal groups returned to their respective lines to announce their decision. Each tribal headsman addressed his people.

"We are your chiefs. It is our responsibility to govern you. We want you to leave this dispute in our hands. We will take care of it. That person who rejects our authority and starts pursuing a different path will bear his burden. Go to your homes quietly.''

There was initial protest, but slowly warriors obeyed; grumbling, they began to disperse. They sat at their homes that afternoon. A few of them continued to shout angry challenges at each other from their respective yards, but by evening all was quiet.

The weeks slipped past. Distant drums still beat out their war messages. Runners still came calling missionaries for sessions of delicate negotiating. But increasingly people turned their attention to the day when they would receive the gift which everybody coveted, but which nobody understood: *dipanda* — independence. Belgian colonial administrators made belated efforts to explain for the people implications of the word. But the fever pitch of nationalism had destroyed all credence in words spoken by colonialists; now their efforts were thought to cloak some deceptive purpose. Congolese derived their own definitions of the word and were believed.

''Spirits of our departed ancestors have sent us a message,'' said some. ''Independence means that we will gain ownership of all the white man's possessions. Clean off our forefathers' neglected grave sites; place on them empty metal chests. On independence morning you'll find them filled with the white man's good things.''

. ''Never before have we been considered persons in our own right,'' said others. ''Do you think the Belgians are going to let all the wealth of this land fall to us now? Nonsense. On independence morning, they're planning to send an armada of planes to drop bombs on us and destroy everything. Then they will leave.''

Suspicion of the Belgians' real intentions fomented fear among blacks. Propagation of the purported message from ancestral spirits fomented anxiety among whites. On the public level, relations between the two races became strained. Members of the white community felt increasingly insecure. White men involved in government, commerce, and industry began sending their wives and children to their overseas homes. Malicious rumors fed fears and spawned a mushrooming evacuation of Europeans.

At Charlesville, missionaries suspected that there might be a rabid black element that wanted to expel them. The arrow shot from ambush had been an early token of it. But Christians in general, and church leaders in particular, affirmed the importance of the continued presence of the missionary.

"People in the villages don't know what is happening around them," leaders would say. "They have no idea what lies before them. So they spread these foolish rumors. God has given us a great responsibility to teach them truth and to bring their minds back into the paths of sanity. For the sake of our church and our new nation, we must be found trustworthy. The pressures brought upon us are powerful, but we will stand. You missionaries must stand with us. Now is when we need you most. If you desert us, we'll see that you never really understood our problems, and never really had our interests at heart. And your leaving would enable Satan to overwhelm us."

Time is heedless of human dilemma; it runs ceaselessly on. Dawn broke on Independence Day, June 30, 1960. Everyone stayed at home, gripped the edges of his seat, and waited with bated breath. Nothing happened. At mid-morning church bells called people to a service of praise and prayer. The braver came. By noon people were milling toward government posts for public festivities celebrating the day. There were parades and dances and contests. There were speeches affirming loving togetherness and promising unlimited progress.

In the late afternoon people went home. They tuned their radios to Leopoldville. People across the country had celebrated quietly. All was under control. President Kasavubu and Prime Minister Lumumba had taken power. Lumumba pointed out that the exodus of Europeans had been pointless; he invited whites who had stayed to join with blacks in building an exemplary African democracy. There was celebrating that night. The men and women of a land had begun to taste the heady potion of human liberty.

A few days passed. The drink began to lose its tang. People recognized that their fallacious dreams were not being fulfilled. They protested what they felt was betrayal. City workers struck, halting functions of transport and government. Soldiers at a key base in western Congo mutinied, demanding the removal of Belgian commanders and higher pay. Lumumba dismissed the white commanders and promised all soldiers pay raises and promotions. But mutineers refused to lay down their arms.

Rampaging soldiers moved into the capital city. They vented their rage not only on Belgian military officers, but on whites in general. They were avenging their people for the abuses they felt they had suffered at the hands of whites for two generations They looted and beat and raped and killed. Terrorized Europeans took flight. The Congo army moved to cut off their escape. Belgium ordered three thousand troops into combat against the Congo army to liberate Belgian citizens.

Rapidly the rebellion spread like a plague across the country. Everywhere the conduct of mutinying soldiers was the same. With the restraining hand of law removed, every man did what was right in his own eyes. In scattered areas, the general population gave vent to long-suppressed feelings and turned against whites. Quarreling tribes resumed their unfinished wars. Kasavubu and Lumumba sped to major troubled areas to restore order, but their appeals went unheeded. Whites began to evacuate en masse. Congo troops took control of key airports and border checkpoints to block their escape. Then the American embassy in Leopoldville announced on radio that it could no longer guarantee the safety of American citizens, and advised them to leave. It was July 9.

Of the two thousand United States citizens in Congo, the majority were missionaries living at an estimated 170 mission stations which dotted the sprawling countryside. The widespread disorder and the radio announcement from the American embassy introduced a painful drama on Charlesville station. Undoubtedly, similar dramas were played on mission stations throughout the country. A decision had to be reached: Should the missionary leave, or should he stay?

Missionaries themselves were divided. Some felt that the presence of the missionary was crucial to the cohesion of society; he should stay even at the risk of life. Others felt that if mutinying troops arrived, trauma of the experience would most seriously affect missionary women and children — they should evacuate; men should stay. Others wondered how a mother could cope with her small children through the unpredictable circumstances of a long exodus that armed soldiers were trying to thwart. Still others felt it hardly noble for a Christian to offer his life in martyrdom when the issue was the color of skin.

Pastor Kazadi was called from Kahemba. He, the missionaries, and the church leaders on the station met for consultation. Missionaries brought the others up-to-date on the spreading disorder and informed them of the embassy message. After a period of weighty deliberation, African leaders reached a basic consensus.

"Things are bad," they said. "There is a big meeting scheduled here in the village this afternoon; the speaker may stir up things further. We are not happy to see you go. But if you stay, and people with bad hearts come to do you evil, we will be obligated to protect you. This could bring harm to us and to our families. You have worked very hard to keep peace among us. When you leave, we don't know what will happen. But it is probably better for you to go."

When one's life has become deeply involved in a people's anguishes and joys, such a precipitant separation produces a deep and painful wrenching. It is like the sudden ripping from the ground of a long-established, deep-rooted plant. Every missionary felt not only the heartsickness of separation. Anxiety weighed like a rock in the pit of his stomach when he recognized that he could be abandoning those he loved to Armageddon.

Suitcases were hastily packed and loaded. Missionaries locked their homes and bade Charlesville church leaders a tearful farewell. They asked Kazadi to bring his family and occupy one of the residences. They left their keys the joint responsibility of the oldest Lulua pastor named Badibanga and the eldest Baluba pastor, Kazadi. Kazadi led in prayer, asking God's protection upon the missionaries for whatever they might encounter ahead. Their trip west by car to firmer footing in a more stable area was the first of several retreats from ever-crumbling ground to their eventual arrival in the United States. The general consensus of missionaries throughout the country was to leave. By the end of July, the number of missionaries residing in Congo plummeted from 1,000 to 147; and of the 114,000 other whites who had once participated in the life of the colony, almost none could be found.

American mission boards with personnel in Congo watched developments there with the closest interest. But their interest was no more avid than that of missionaries preparing to return. Archie and Irma Graber and their daughter, Nancy, were in America completing their furlough. It was the evening of July 10. They had been anticipating this day for months. They drove a new five-ton Chevrolet truck onto the parking lot of the Evangelical Mennonite Church at Berne, Indiana. The truck was loaded high with missionary personnel effects and supplies to strengthen the work at Kalonda station; the load was covered with a tight-drawn tarpaulin. This was Irma's home church. They would have the farewell service tonight and proceed toward the East Coast in the morning. They greeted the pastor and made preparations for the service. Irma and Nancy went to sit in a front pew of the sanctuary. There was a crowd of about three hundred. Archie and the pastor waited at a side door to go onto the platform. Suddenly an usher arrived and handed Archie a note.

He read: "Your mission board just called. They received word from Congo today that things there are getting much worse and that the Graber family should not come."

16

... The Sky Is Falling ...

GRABER IMPROVISED HIS message before a stunned but sympathetic audience. The next day he and his family took up temporary residence in a basement apartment at mission headquarters in Elkhart, Indiana, to await some further directive. Stories of the Congo crisis began making international headlines. Archie read the daily installments with growing alarm. For him, the effects such events were having on black people he dearly loved could only be speculated. For those caught in the throes of these events, their effects were terrifyingly real.

For all of living memory, the Congolese had learned to build their existence upon a social order that was stable. That stability accrued from combined forces of which the white man was progenitor. He governed them. He ran businesses among them. He managed industry. He curbed their epidemic diseases. He preached the gospel. To the Congo peoples, these forces constituted pillars that supported the four corners of their world. Then suddenly, when the white man was removed from the scene, the pillars crumbled. The precipitous departure of whites and the mutiny of armed forces left a void open to lawlessness.

The province of Kasai, hinterland home of the Lulua, the Baluba, and smaller adjacent tribes, had long suffered endemic intertribal tensions. Now it became the scene of Congo's most violent disorders. Immediately upon the heels of the white evacuation and the military mutiny, tribal fighting broke out at Charlesville, Tshikapa, Luluabourg, and at a dozen other points within the province. Tribes would join forces, defeat a common enemy, and then break their alliance to turn against each other. Such splintering and resplintering of loyalties gradually disintegrated civil order. War raged unchecked, until its vanquished were driven away as impoverished refugees. Individuals, unrestrained by law, took to violently avenging personal grievances. Christians witnessed scenes they would one day recount: an infant held by the ankles and clubbed against a tree; a decapitated human body that ran twenty yards before it collapsed. Unrelentingly, a society slipped into the lowering darkness of barbarism.

Anarchy was not universal. Disorders in the country's southeastern province of Katanga were largely confined to its northwestern frontier, where it bordered Kasai. On July 14 the Katanga legislature voted for Katanga to secede from Congo, and appointed Moise Tshombe its president. Katanga held about three-fourth's of Congo's known mineral wealth. For mutual benefit, Katanga and Belgium reaffirmed their alliance, and over eight thousand Belgian troops joined Katangese forces to maintain order.

Breaking with the Congo Central Government was the plan not only of leaders in Katanga. On August 8 Albert Kalonji, whose arrest had triggered Baluba rioting in preindependence days, announced that he was reestablishing a Baluba kingdom in his tribe's ancient tribal homeland in southeastern Kasai. Its capital city would be Bakwanga. He appealed for all Baluba, driven as refugees from the four corners of the land, to come find shelter there and to help him. This announcement fed animosity against the Baluba and heightened the intensity of war to uproot them. Scores of thousands of Baluba refugees began converging on their ancestral homeland called ''South Kasai.'' Kalonji's intention soon became clear: to secede from Congo, to become an independent sovereign state with close ties to bordering Katanga.

Meanwhile the Congo problem was on center-stage at the United Nations in New York City. Russia's unilateral decision to support Lumumba produced a major crisis in East-West relations. The United Nations decided that massive intervention was the only way to reduce the threat of world war. In spite of recurring disputes over sovereign rights between U.N. Secretary Dag Hammarskjold and Congo's ruling heads in Leopoldville, by the end of July 1960, twelve thousand U.N. ''Blue Helmets'' from nine countries were working in Congo to restore order.

Congo's Prime Minister Lumumba knew that revenue from Katanga minerals and South Kasai diamonds was crucial to the survival of his government. When the U.N. Command refused to send its troops against secessionist Katanga, Lumumba drew up an alternative plan. He decided to send Congo troops against the Baluba of South Kasai to terminate the secessionist ambitions of Albert Kalonji; then the capital city of Bakwanga could be used as a supply point for his troops to launch an invasion south into secessionist Katanga.

The decision of Lumumba to send his troops against the Baluba kingdom had tribal undercurrents which could only add to the ferocity of the conflict. In the 1890s, a cannibalistic tribal predecessor to Lumumba named Ngongo Lutete had made two slave raids against the Baluba, which decimated the tribe.[1] They remembered the horrible cruelties their grandfathers had suffered at that man's hands then; how could they ever bow to one of his descendants now? When Lumumba was snubbed by the United Nations, he turned for help to the Russians. Soon Ilyushin-14 transports were flying Russian trucks and Congo troops to Luluabourg to launch from there the invasion of South Kasai.

Congo army troops traveling by road reached the border of Baluba land. Population of the province was swelling with the daily arrival of refugees. For them, to the blight of famine was now added the plight of war. Troops entered the province, met scattered resistance in villages, quickly suppressed it, and moved on to the capital city of Bakwanga. There the battle was joined. Fighting between Congo troops and Baluba tribesmen supporting Kalonji flared into a no-quarter war of terrible ferocity, "unprecedented even for the Congo, where savagery is nothing new," with women and children among its victims.[2]

Reports of such events remain cold and impersonal until we understand how these events affect human beings. Paul Mukendi was the son of Luaba, the Baluba pastor so close to Archie Graber during his early years at Charlesville. Mukendi's case is typical of Baluba people living at that time in the provincial capital city of Luluabourg. For them, there was harassment. There were threats. There were night attacks on their homes. Eventually life became so intolerable they had no alternative but to leave. For some, coveted possessions so arduously collected through the years were destroyed when their homes were burned. For others,

---

[1] See Levi Keidel, *Black Samson* (Carol Stream, IL: Creation House, 1975), chaps. 2,3.
[2] United Press International wire service report of 4 September 1960.

hard decisions had to be made about what to take and what to abandon. Some form of the following scene was played in every Baluba home yet unscathed by war.

"Will we need to leave our dining table and chairs?" the wife asked.

"How would they find place on a truck full of refugees?" the husband replied.

"What about my pretty dinner-table dishes?"

"Let's try to put everything we want to take along into our big, metal storage chest. First put into it blankets, cooking pans, and clothing for us and the children. Then if there is still room, you can put in the table dishes."

"What will we sleep on when we get there if we don't take our bed?"

"When this trouble is finished, a carpenter can make another bedframe for us. But we spent a lot of money for the mattress. We'll try to take it along."

While she packed, he rode his bicycle into the city, braving the hostile looks of Lulua who recognized him. He visited a succession of points where transport trucks regularly arrived and departed. On the second or third day he found a trader with a truck scheduled to make the fifty-mile trip to the border of South Kasai. He reserved space for himself and his family.

Then followed the task of transporting their remaining personal effects to the point of departure. Sometimes arrangements could be made with a non-Lulua taxi driver. Sometimes it meant hauling the packed metal chest and the tied mattress in a borrowed wheelbarrow. Finally the moment came to leave their home. In the backyard sat a large, white enamel basin piled high with final essentials, wrapped into a bundle with a heavy blanket knotted at the top. The wife stooped low to tie her baby onto her back with a sturdy waistcloth. Then the husband helped her lift the loaded basin onto her head. He went first, pushing a bicycle and carrying perhaps a thermos jug or a shiny pressure lantern. She followed with the basin, her baby, and a toddler clinging to her hand on either side.

They arrived in time. But as the truck was taking its load, other refugees arrived. They frantically pleaded for space. Others feared losing their places. Confusion mounted to virtual bedlam. Seating boards were removed to allow more space. Arguing broke out about what was to be loaded.

"Step aside for me to load this chest."

"What do you mean loading your *things* when there are *people* who want to go?"

"But I paid the chauffeur to haul these things. You think I'm going to leave them now?"

"Don't you know tribesmen here want to kill us? Are you going to leave your kinsmen here to die so that you can take your *things?*"

"Here," the chauffeur said, intervening, "take back the money you gave me to haul your things. Things can be replaced. When people die, they are lost forever. Climb into the truck."

"On the afternoon of August 12, my wife, our four small children and I found space in a big Ford truck," Mukendi recalled. "We left everything behind. We didn't even have a cooking pot. We had only a blanket to help keep the children warm. The chauffeur was from a neutral tribe; no one here had a score to settle with him. Most of us paid him. Some refugees came who had no money. They wept and pleaded, and he put them in for nothing. He kept putting in people until we were like matches in a box. Behind the truck the yard was full of piles of valuable things: mattresses, bicycles, blanket-bound basins, chests. We were abandoning them. We all knew that warriors from villages along the road were ambushing truckloads of refugees. Everybody was afraid. In our hearts we were all pleading with God to have mercy on us. The chauffeur closed us up under a tarpaulin so passersby could not see that he was hauling people. Then we began our journey. A few miles out of Luluabourg we came to the last Baluba village, and stopped.

" 'How are things ahead?' the chauffeur asked.

" 'There's fighting at the first river bridge. You can't get through. Stay here until that fighting is finished. Then some morning you can start out again, and pass through in daylight.'

"We stayed there for two days. Village people shared their food with us. On the third morning we left. We passed through unfriendly villages without trouble, and crossed the border into South Kasai. We kept traveling until evening, when we reached Miabi, a village at a crossroads. Before the disorders it had not been a big village. But now we found that 3,000 refugees had arrived there ahead of us. They were building huts here and there, wherever they found a place. Many hundreds had no shelter; some of them could not build their own huts; they were too weak with hunger. These hundreds were sleeping with their children outside on the ground.

"The village people welcomed us warmly. 'You can sit here, and build your homes, and make your gardens,' they said. 'We did not know that this number of refugees would come here. Their great number has depleted the food we have in our fields. But we will share with you what little we have.'

"We found friends who took us to a little hut where we could sit and rest. During the following days my wife and I spent much of our time scraping together bits of food we could find here and there to reduce the crying of the children.

"Then one day soldiers came. They said Chief Kalonji had sent them to guard us and to help us find food. They sat with us two days. On the third day they began catching and beating people. They had lied to us. They were not sent by Kalonji. They were sent by Lumumba. Fighting broke out. Many people died. We watched them die with our own eyes. I took my wife and children. We fled into the forest to hide. We stayed there four days, but hunger-suffering surpassed us. We returned to the village. The soldiers were gone. People were dying from hunger. Children were dying in great numbers. Everybody was wasting away, because there was no food."

Unknown to Mukendi and to the scores of thousands he represented, compassionate people were moving to help them. In early August, Orie Miller, a veteran with forty years of experience in war-relief operations, came from the Mennonite Central Committee in Akron, Pennsylvania, to Leopoldville to survey needs and to outline strategy for meeting them. He met with a skeleton staff of missionaries still residing in the city. On August 17 they organized the Congo Protestant Relief Agency (CPRA) for the purpose of alleviating human suffering in strife-torn areas of the country. On August 20–22 Miller and AIMM missionary Robert Bontrager, chairman of CPRA, flew to Bakwanga, South Kasai, to gain a firsthand understanding of the scope of the crisis there. They found an estimated 180,000 to 250,000 dispossessed refugees with another 100,000 expected imminently. The mass suffering and death they witnessed prompted Bontrager to call it "one of the world's worst famines in modern times."[3]

[3] "The Hungry Country," *Congo Missionary Messenger,* April 1961, p. 10.

Refugees fleeing to South Kasai *(WCC)*

Planning relief efforts in Bakwanga: (from left) Archie Graber; Orie Miller, co-founder of CPRA; and Dr. Loenstein, a U.N. nutrition expert

A burned-out hut in a Baluba village destroyed by Lulua

Archie, Irma, and daughter Nancy at plane as Archie returns to the Congo

Miller had organized many relief operations before. But this one had its own set of problems. Given the turbulent political conditions, who were the government authorities to work through? South Kasai was geographically isolated. It was at war with the central government; it was bordered on the west by enemy Lulua; and war was disrupting transport lines across its southern frontier with friendly Katanga. By what means could relief supplies be brought into the country? With sporadic outbreaks of war in the province, how could there be organized distribution of relief supplies which did arrive?

Gripped by the overwhelming dimension of human need, they discounted the seemingly formidable obstacles and joined themselves in a race against starvation. Miller returned to the States to mobilize the efforts of relief agencies.[4] Bontrager sent with Miller a letter addressed to AIMM home secretary Vernon Sprunger with a special request.

The day the letter arrived at the home office in Elkhart, Indiana, had been like any other day for Archie Graber. He had been doing carpentry work in the new home of a friend. When he came from work that evening, he was called into Sprunger's office.

"The Congo Protestant Relief Agency sent Bontrager and Miller to Bakwanga to visit the Baluba refugees," Sprunger said. "Some of your old friends from Charlesville are here. They are asking you to come help them. They say you could help bring an end to their wilderness wanderings and get them settled in the land of their forefathers. The CPRA is asking you to come head up its relief efforts to the Baluba refugees in South Kasai. The Mennonite Central Committee is offering to provide your financial support."

Graber felt honored that his black friends had chosen him.

"Why wouldn't my tribemates choose Lutonga?" Kazadi asked later. "His mind was that of a black elder who knows how to help any other black person. His skin was white, but he had become our flesh and blood. Our fathers used to say, 'Wherever you are, and however you suffer, the nape of your neck will always follow you.'"

"How do you feel about it?" Sprunger asked Graber.

"Why, I feel it's the call of God."

[4]Groups cooperating in the relief effort of CPRA included Church World Service, Mennonite Central Committee, Evangelical Foreign Missions Association, Christian Medical Society, International Foreign Missions Association, World Vision, and the Agriculture Technical Assistance Foundation.

Archie settled his wife and daughter in an apartment in Fort Wayne, Indiana. On Friday, September 2, the United Nations Command in Congo reported a fresh outbreak of fighting at Bakwanga between the forces of Prime Minister Lumumba and those of King Kalonji. On that same day, Archie packed a suitcase, drove with his wife and daughter to Toledo, Ohio, said good-by to them, and boarded a plane on his way to South Kasai to help his friends.

Part 3

... Bitter Harvest ...

17

... Wretched Reunion ...

GRABER'S FLIGHT TO Congo was normal until the plane was crossing high over northwest Africa. There, during the early morning hours of September 4, the pilot learned that runways of the Leopoldville airport were blocked with fifty-gallon drums. He diverted the flight southward into bordering Portuguese Angola, to the city of Luanda. There he disembarked his passengers. All normal entryways into Congo were closed; only United Nations planes were allowed to land at the Leopoldville airport. Four days later Graber boarded a United Nations two-motor cargo plane loaded with smelly dried fish, slipped into the country, and landed at Leopoldville on a partially blocked runway.

He went into the city and took a room at a missionary hostel. Then he met with CPRA authorities. They helped him secure a residence visa and official government papers asking military personnel manning roadblocks throughout the country to allow him to circulate freely. They laid strategy for securing relief supplies and for transporting them nine hundred miles inland to the mecca toward which unnumbered thousands of Baluba refugees were converging — Bakwanga, South Kasai.

At that time the only corridor open for shipping supplies to the Baluba kingdom was from the South Atlantic ocean port of Lobito, by rail across the country of Portuguese Angola, then north through Tshombe's break-off Congo province of Katanga, and into bordering South Kasai. Archie flew to Lobito and arranged for rail-shipping 150 tons of rice, which had already arrived there. He returned to Leopoldville and made reservations on a commercial flight to Luluabourg, eight hundred miles inland, for October 1. From there he hoped to make local arrangements for the remaining ninety-mile trip east to Bakwanga.

It would take more than Graber's enthusiasm to carry out a program of relief. He had to work within the context of erratic Congo politics. When troops sent by Premier Lumumba reached Bakwanga, they took over the airport. Reenforcements were flown in to join them. A local incident triggered fighting between Lumumba's troops and warriors supporting separatist King Kalonji. The troops were armed with modern weapons; the Baluba warriors with homemade shotguns. A brief engagement produced a blood bath. Baluba resistance was wiped out, and Kalonji fled into exile in Katanga. Lumumba's troops proceeded south to launch an invasion into break-off Katanga. For food they lived off the land. For transportation, they commandeered whatever vehicles they could find.

Congo President Kasavubu and General of the Army Mobutu shared Lumumba's purpose to reintegrate the break-off provinces, but they were displeased by his method. Then they were angered when Lumumba began importing trucks and supplies from Communist-bloc nations across a northern frontier directly into Kasai, in violation of the United Nations mandate to maintain peace. Lumumba's fortunes plummeted. Reports of the massacre of Baluba in South Kasai reached army troops of Baluba origin stationed near Leopoldville. They rioted. Screaming for Lumumba's blood, they attacked a barracks where he was spending the night. A Ghanian contingent of U.N. troops intervened, rescued Lumumba, and held him in protective custody over the protests of General Mobutu.

In mid-September Kasavubu called a cease-fire in Kasai and Katanga. He purposed to settle the problem of secession by negotiation rather than by force. Mobutu ordered troops back to their bases. U.N. planes provided their transportation. With the pressure off, Balubu leader Kalonji returned from exile to Bakwanga to reestablsih his regime. He recruited Belgian military officers to train and command his troops; together they would protect diamond mine operations there. He gave the Belgian mining company its share of diamond revenue and used the balance to run his government and to pay air fares for returning

Baluba refugees. He charged Lumumba with "murder, kidnappings, and rape," and demanded that Central Government authorities bring him to justice.

Such was the political context when Graber flew to Luluabourg on his way to South Kasai to launch a relief program. Enroute he received three letters from Baluba King Kalonji, president of South Kasai Province, inviting him to come help the refugees. On October 4 a Presbyterian missionary flew him the last leg of the trip to Bakwanga. Archie stepped off the little plane, picked up his two suitcases, walked across the tarmac, and entered the small terminal building. He was a stranger among strangers. He could not at that moment have even imagined that after a few short years of his ministry, hundreds of thousands of these strangers would revere his name. Such a possibility was even more remote from his thinking when he began to absorb the ghastly devastation around him.

He contacted diamond mine officials. They gave him lodging in their motellike guesthouse. Of the usual 180 European mine supervisors, all but 30 had fled. These 30 were still recovering from the trauma of the recent attack by the troops of Lumumba. Food, blankets, and other merchandise worth almost a million dollars had been looted from their stores. All but forty of the company's four hundred vehicles had been confiscated by Lumumba's soldiers, driven until wrecked or out of gas, and abandoned.

Two remaining company doctors lived in fear of an outbreak of epidemic, which they would be powerless to control. The original Baluba population of about one millin had lived largely on subsistence agriculture. When army troops of Lumumba passed through the land, they depleted all food reserves. To this burden were added the needs of an estimated 250,000 refugees. Other thousands were still coming. Starvation already stalked the land; it was claiming some 200 lives daily.

Graber learned that a European mine official named Jackmay planned a ninety-mile trip to Mwena Ditu,[1] a railroad town on the southwest frontier of the province. The town was a transport lifeline for South Kasai . . . the only point for rail-shipping goods in and out of the break-away province. He seized the opportunity to go along. This trip would give Archie some firsthand knowledge of the scope of human

---

[1]Pronounced Mway-nah Dee-too

need. Also, he could try to trace the whereabouts of that 150 tons of rice he had shipped from Lobito. He did not foresee that after this journey he would never be the same.

They left the city and took a gravel road south. The landscape grew more and more bleak and deserted. Here was a burned-out abandoned village. There was the blackened hulk of an abandoned automobile. Approaching them on foot was a refugee family . . . a man pushing an overloaded bicycle . . . a woman steadying a great burden on her head with one hand, leading a small child with the other, and carrying an infant bound by a waistcloth to her back . . . a stooped shriveled old woman with a tiny basin of personal effects balanced on her head, pulling herself onward by careful, measured steps assisted by a crooked walking stick.

About fifteen miles south of Bakwanga the car made a turn to the right. Suddenly Graber saw corpses scattered on both sides of the road.

"Roll up your window fast," Jackmay said. "Keep out the flies and the smell. This is the village of Tshilenge. About a month ago Lumumba's troops and Kalonji's warriors tangled here. They say about four hundred were killed. Henry Taylor, a Scripps-Howard reporter, was killed here."

Closed windows kept out the flies, but not the smell. Neither could Graber shut out the visual images. For miles his eyes caught chilling symbols . . . shoes and shredded clothing strewn along the roadside . . . corpses hastily covered with loose dirt . . . a broken spear. For mile after mile the images of horror kept repeating themselves . . . the wrecked hulks of vehicles . . . the burned and leveled villages . . . decaying corpses. He was numbed with shock. His head began to swim. It was a scene lifted out of Dante's *Inferno*, the endless line of straggling refugees were the tormented, passing silently, heedlessly, like preprogramed robots, across this scarred, fetid wasteland.

Reporting his experience sometime later, Graber graphically described what he saw in that part of the country. "The entire town of Luputa was destroyed," he wrote. "Buildings of cement block were still standing, but doors and windows were broken. Hundreds of people were sitting on the ground in the hot sun, with little piles of things they could get away with lying near them. They were hungry. Their babies were crying. Filth, flies, and sickness were everywhere. Those people sat hoping for a way to leave that place of horror. Many others were hiding in the forest, afraid to go to their fields for food. Everything these people had was stolen or destroyed by pillaging soldiers.''

In Mwena Ditu he found fewer buildings destroyed, but the human toll was much the same. What bothered him most was the picture of suffering children — their puffy eyes, bronze-colored hair, bloated tummies, and broomstick limbs. Children and old people sat or lay in the dust, scattered here and there, like living skeletons, numb and silent from shock, staring emptily into space. They couldn't join the trek of refugees. They couldn't go anywhere. They were waiting . . . waiting either for someone to bring them food or for slow death by starvation. Graber was a compassionate man. His powerlessness to relate to such human suffering left him almost physically ill.

He was able to rent a large warehouse. But the 150-ton shipment of rice he hoped to store in it was delayed. In a war-torn area rails had been lifted; train service from the south into Mwena Ditu was interrupted indefinitely.

Archie returned to his guest room in Bakwanga. Old Christian friends from his years at Charlesville heard by the grapevine that Lutonga had arrived. They came to see him, and there was a joyous reunion. Then they pieced together for him a picture of the horror they had endured.

"The Industrial School building here in Bakwanga was packed with refugees . . . men, women, and children," they said. "When the soldiers came, they killed every one of them. They killed patients in the hospital, and mothers and babies in the maternity ward; there was nothing left living. At school they machine-gunned our children while they tried to hide behind their desks. After it all passed, we stacked our dead like pieces of firewood."

When Graber recovered from the trauma of those first days, he began to ask himself some questions. Had anything during his thirty years in Congo prepared him for this? He had always been an evangelistic missionary, calling people to Christ. He had no experience in feeding the hungry. Why had God brought him here? What amount of effort could ever heal such brokenness? Empty-handed, without experience, and in the face of such appalling need, what could he do? The little boy who helped Jesus feed the five thousand at least had five loaves. Graber didn't have a crumb.

One thing was certain. The condition of the refugees was so

deplorable that he could not desert them. In kinder times he had brought them the message of salvation. Now he had to stay with them to prove to them that God hadn't forgotten them. And if he was going to stay, it was senseless to do nothing. He had to believe that God had moved men to organize CPRA . . . that God had brought him here . . . that God would remove the seemingly formidable obstacles. If he really believed these things, he could only move ahead.

His priority need was a large quantity of food. He wrote CPRA headquarters in Leopoldville ordering 100 tons of rice and 100 tons of beans per month, 500 sacks of salt, 100,000 blankets, and 2 large transport trucks; he asked them to send additional personnel — a veteran missionary to help him manage the program and two young men who could handle the trucks. He secured a $5,000 donation from the Presbyterian mission working in the area and ordered supplies available in Luluabourg . . . 20 tons of manioc flour, 35 tons of corn meal, 150 cases of medicated soap, and 30 tons of corn. He prayed desperately that somehow God would open the way for food to arrive soon.

He needed more than food. He needed transportation. He was footsore from walking around town. Until the trucks he had ordered arrived, how could he transport relief supplies to towns throughout the province where refugees were converging and where the starving sat waiting? His first hope for a means of transportation came with an unexpected visitor.

During the night of October 8 Archie was aroused by a knock on the door. He turned on the light and looked at his watch. It was five minutes before midnight. He was suspicious of any caller this time of night.

"Who's there?" he called.

"I'm Henry Crane from the Presbyterian mission."

Henry was an old acquaintance of Archie. He was a man already acquainted with the horror of war; he had lost an eye during the Battle of the Bulge in World War II. Graber got up and let him in. His face was drained and lined from tension and fatigue.

"What's happened, Hank?"

"I was trying to come here from Luluabourg by road. When I got to the tribal border line at Lake Munkamba, I was held up there by three of King Kalonji's soldiers. When I got out of the car, they turned three machine guns at me and asked to see my credentials. I showed them all my papers. They weren't satisfied. They were looking for some kind of pass from Kalonji. They accused me of being an advance spy for a detachment of Central Government soldiers they said was following me. They searched my car inside and out, but didn't find anything. They said I had to go with them to police headquarters here in Bakwanga. They shoved me into their car and held loaded machine guns on me the full forty-five miles of rough road. We arrived here about ten. They took me to a military justice. I pled with the man there for almost two hours before he finally accepted my story and released me.''

Archie secretly wondered when his turn would come.

"Thank God you're still alive," he said. "What can I do for you?"

"I left the chauffeur out there guarding my station wagon. I have to go back in the morning. U.N. soldiers are escorting me. If you want to go along, you can bring the station wagon back and use it for your relief program."

"Thank you, Hank. It will sure come in handy."

At 8:45 the following morning, two white U.N. diesel trucks and a jeep arrived. The trucks were loaded with forty armed Tunisian soldiers. Graber and Crane climbed with the commanding officer into the chauffeured jeep. They traveled between the two armed trucks and arrived at Lake Munkamba without incident. Crane's chauffeur was still there guarding the station wagon.

"Did you have any trouble?" Hank asked him.

"No. Almost all night I stayed with the car. Near morning I went to a nearby hut to sleep a little."

Crane got into the driver's seat and ground the starter. The motor wouldn't fire. There was a pause.

"The gas guage says the tank is empty," he called to Graber. "When could someone have stolen the gas?" he asked the chauffeur.

"If someone stole the gas, they had to do it during the short time I was sleeping."

There was no way of transferring gas from the jeep. Crane told the chauffeur to stay with the car until they returned. The caravan bounced the forty-five miles back to Bakwanga, got gas, and returned to Lake Munkamba. The station wagon and the chauffeur had vanished. No one around offered a clue as to what had happened to them. The caravan returned to Bakwanga and dropped Archie off at home. It had been a long day, and the problem of transportation was no nearer a solution.

Every day seems endless when you live among mounting numbers of starving people and are powerless to help them. Archie felt it was still a long way to the day he would launch a feeding program. He gained an interview with Prime Minister Ngalula, who served under President Kalonji, and was promised help with transportation. But Graber knew well how quickly government officials could forget promises. He spent three weeks of those long days at Bakwanga. He began wondering if God still noticed him. Then his first break came. It was a note from the railroad company: "Four carloads of rice arriving at Mwena Ditu Sunday."

18

... Assault on Famine ...

ARCHIE CAUGHT A ride to the railroad town on the following Tuesday, October 25. He took up temporary residence with a Belgian businessman named Swaenen, his wife, and their two children, who lived in the back part of a store they operated there. The rice shipment had arrived. The cars had been broken into, but only sixty-nine of the three thousand bags of rice were missing. By evening Graber had rented two local transport trucks.

Next morning he hired forty-seven local workmen. They began unloading the rice from the railroad cars and hauling it to the warehouse. The men worked well. During the day two carloads of corn and manioc flour arrived. Graber was encouraged. The program was beginning to inch forward. At last he had something to give these starving people. Word got around that he would be distributing food. By mid-afternoon about a thousand people were waiting for rice. Graber was inside a railroad car helping load a truck when he heard men yelling something outside. Workmen in the truck listened and froze in fear.

"What's the matter?" he asked.

"It's war."

"Where?"

"Tribal enemies have attacked one of our villages twelve miles from here. They've set it on fire. Preacher, we're leaving."

"Why are you leaving? Don't you see all these hungry people here waiting for food?"

"We are at war, preacher. We're going to our homes. We'll help our wives and children get ready to flee to the forest to hide. We may need to help fight.''

It was clear that these men were fiercely proud of their autonomy as a separate Baluba kingdom; they were ready to stand with Kalonji's soldiers to fight for it. There was nothing for Graber to do but to close down his hauling operation, return to the Swaenens, and await the outcome of things.

Next morning word leaked back of what had happened. Three villages and a Catholic seminary had been burned by invading tribesmen. Many Congolese and a Belgian priest had been killed. A U.N. doctor was shot three times in the legs and hand. Four Liberian U.N. soldiers were wounded. Only a few workmen showed up for duty that morning. Graber did what he could with a limited staff to unload the rice all that day and returned to the Belgian businessman's home for the night.

After supper that evening, Archie was relaxing inside the house. Suddenly, at 7:30, shooting broke out. ''Soldiers began shooting around us on all four sides,'' Graber reported later. ''A machine gun was shooting from an emplacement less than a hundred feet from where Swaenen, his family, and I were trying to hide. We turned out the lights and waited. Heaven seemed much nearer than Fort Wayne, Indiana, just then.'' Shooting subsided about nine o'clock. They passed an uneasy night. Archie was certain no worker would show up in the morning.

Shortly after daybreak they peeked out the windows. The streets were empty. There was no sign of dead, or of wounded, or of fresh destruction. All was at peace. By the time they had eaten breakfast, people were passing along the streets going about their duties. Graber went to the warehouse. The workmen had reported full force. He couldn't figure it out.

''I'm happy you've come,'' he said to them.

''You've given us work to do. Why shouldn't we come?''

''I don't understand. When there is a war twelve miles away, you leave the work and run. When war comes to your town, you all come to work.''

''War?'' They looked at each other questioningly. ''What war?''

''All that shooting last night.''

They laughed. ''That wasn't war, preacher. Soldiers of King

Kalonji had just returned from the war of the day before. They were celebrating their victory."

The men could handle the unloading of the railroad cars that day without him, Archie decided. He put a supply of rice in a nearby room and began distributing it to the hungry. He had never handled a crowd of hungry people before. He had only a tin cup to use as a measure for everybody. At first the people were orderly and quiet, each one awaiting his turn. Gradually the crowd grew to an impatient, pressing throng. A mother begged for a second tinful for her family of five children. People behind her shouted angrily for her to move on. Fear that there would not be enough food to go around transformed the crowd into a surging, hunger-crazed mob. It pressed forward, went out of control, broke through the doorway, and stampeded the supply room. Graber escaped through a rear window. When he returned later, he found the room cleaned out down to a spoonful of rice grains.

A few days later he wrote from Bakwanga, "I returned from troubled Mwena Ditu last night. It was a hard week. I supervised the unloading of six carloads of rice and gave rations to 6,500 people. I am so glad to be back on the field. Never in my life have I experienced anything like this."

There was good news awaiting him at Bakwanga. CPRA staff in Leopoldville had found ways to ship some supplies directly to Bakwanga by air — in extra space on a Red Cross plane or on planes Kalonji had chartered to haul Baluba refugees. First came powdered milk — 5½ tons on one plane, then 2¼ tons on another. Two young Americans, Allen Horst and Abe Suderman, who had been doing relief work in Europe under the Mennonite Central Committee, were transferred to Bakwanga to help Graber. Prime Minister Ngalula came through on his promise to help with transportation; the Kalonji government loaned Archie two six-ton Mercedes-Benz diesel trucks. A large-caliber bullet hole on the driver's side of one was a mute reminder that they lived in a society on the brink of crisis.

Horst and Suderman drove one of the trucks into a devastated no man's land separating two warring tribes and towed out a stripped, abandoned Volkswagen minibus given them by the Presbyterian mission. They restored its stolen parts, installed a new motor, and put it into service again. Graber rejoiced. He painted a large CPRA insignia on the sides of the three vehicles to link his relief work with the church. He wanted to make sure the glory of his efforts went to the Lord. At long last he could launch a feeding program.

Archie decided that the point of most crucial need was twenty miles west of Bakwanga at the crossroads town of Miabi, to which Paul Mukendi (son of Charlesville pastor Luaba) and his family had fled in August. On November 11 Graber hauled in rice and powdered milk and set up a feeding center there.

Refugees had exploded the town's normal population of about 2,000 to 30,000. The long, low, cement-block, barracks-type buildings of the 250-bed hospital there were crowded with sick and dying to perhaps five times their normal capacity. Children, many like skeletons, but with grossly distended stomachs, were lying four and five to a bed. The number of ill lying on mats on the ward floors hardly allowed for walking space between them. For many of the patients, the hospital was only a shelter to which they had come to die. A single medical assistant with practically no medicines was in charge. Orie Miller, with forty years of experience in world-wide relief work, called it "as pitiful a sight of human misery and suffering from lack of food and medical care as I have ever seen."[1]

Graber's experience at Mwena Ditu had taught him that feeding operations must be organized. He would have to hire responsible people to help him. The Kalonji government had promised to cover their salaries. He had designed a ration card and had a quantity of them printed. At Miabi he hired a dozen local Christians to help him. Some worked as secretaries; they filled out a ration card for the head of each family needing food. Others distributed rice. Using tin-can measures, they gave each family head presenting a ration card four pounds . . . enough to last for a week.

Others mixed powdered milk; they gave each child in turn a vitamin pill and a cup of milk, and saw to it that they were taken on the spot. On the first day of distribution, four thousand people each received a week's ration of food and two thousand children received a vitamin pill and milk. After the feeding center was opened, the staff gave children milk and vitamins daily. On the appointed day weekly, CPRA trucks brought ten tons of food to Miabi for distribution to family heads and returned to Bakwanga with any balance.

Another point of appalling need was at Lake Munkamba, forty-five

[1]Diary note of Orie O. Miller, *CPRA News Sheet* No. 8 (10 January 1961).

Congolese boy stands beside a CPRA truck bringing food to Baluba refugees. *(AIMM)*

Young and old bear the marks of hunger. A grandmother and two girls come to meet the CPRA truck. *(MCC)*

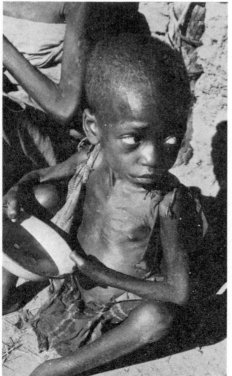

A young victim of the nutritional disease kwashiorkor *(WCC)*

Archie Graber, with a CPRA truck, receives a load of food from a United Nations plane. *(MCC)*

A caravan of trucks bringing food to refugees

Hungry Congolese await meal distribution in South Kasai famine area. (AIMM)

Children in the Baluba camp *(WCC)*

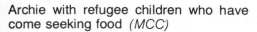

Archie with refugee children who have come seeking food *(MCC)*

Mother and child suffering from tuberculosis *(MCC)*

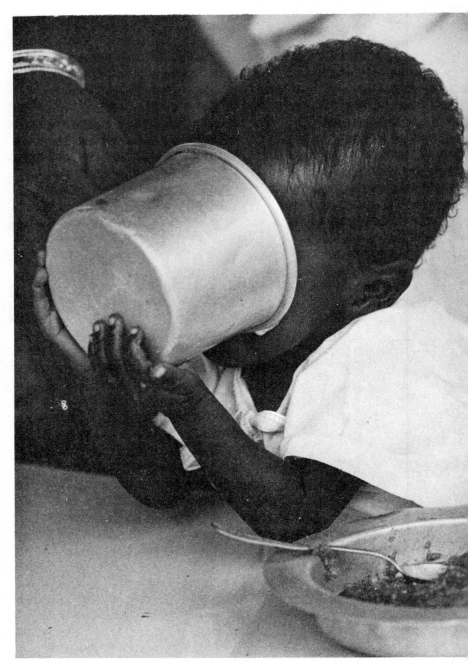

A long-awaited meal *(MCC)*

miles west of Bakwanga, where Graber had gone with Henry Crane in the hope of getting a car. The borders of three tribal areas converged there — the Lulua to the west, the Baluba to the east, and the Luntu, a small combative tribe, to the north. The area was torn by periodic warfare. Baluba refugees spilled across its borders into South Kasai daily. Here Archie set up the second feeding center.

A refugee settlement, called Cha Cha Cha, sprawled for five miles along the road just east of Lake Munkamba. Archie planned a trip to take food there. Rev. Isaac Kanyinda, an acquaintance of Graber from his years at Tshikapa, wanted to go along. Kanyinda had pastored a large Presbyterian church in Luluabourg. When fighting broke out there, he hid in the tall prairie grass in Lulua country for twenty-eight days before he escaped. Now he was concerned for his brother, Muamba. "I think I'll find him at Cha Cha Cha," Kanyinda said. "He's been a Christian for many years. His wife is a Lulua; she deserted him. He needs help badly. If I find him, I want to bring him with us to Bakwanga to be with our parents here."

Archie helped load a truck and the CPRA minibus with fifty sacks of corn meal. He, Kanyinda, and a truck driver drove to the settlement. On viewing the situation, Archie was convinced that a third of the children would die within six months unless food and medicine reached them. Kanyinda found his brother. Archie unloaded the minibus, drove it up the road to the appointed hut, and got out to help. The man was lying on a mat beneath a shelter. Kanyinda lifted him to his feet and helped him to the vehicle.

"Can't he walk?" Archie asked.

"He hasn't been eating," the pastor replied. "There has been no food here."

They helped the sick man into the rear of the minibus; Kanyinda got in and sat on the floor beside him. Archie climbed into the driver's seat, and they started on their way back to Bakwanga. About six miles down the road Kanyinda's voice rose in a rending wail.

"My brother Muamba. My brother Muamba. He's dead. He's dead," the pastor mourned.

Archie glanced to the rear. Kanyinda's tear-streaked face was lifted heavenward, his eyes closed, his hand pressed to his forehead, his shoulders heaving with sobs. Archie gripped the wheel and stared down the road, stricken with grief, debating what to do. Finally he stopped.

He went to the right side of the vehicle, opened the door, and waited until the sobbing subsided.

"Pastor," he asked, "what would it be good for us to do?"

The black man looked at Graber pensively, his face wet and sad.

"His soul has already gone to be with God," he said. "We may as well bury him here."

They wrapped the body in two reed mats. Under a lone, roadside palm tree they dug a grave and buried Muamba. Kanyinda, kneeling beside the fresh-heaped earth, began choking back sobs. Graber stood watching. *O God,* he cried in his heart, *is there no way to bring enough food to stop this dying?*

It was difficult for Archie to communicate his sense of shock and horror through CPRA headquarters to Christians in Europe and North America. But eventually the message got through, and, as reported in a release by United Press International, "the wheels of organized compassion began to move." Christians in Switzerland sent money to buy 20,000 blankets. Denmark flew in a plane-load of milk. West German churches sent 700 tents. Belgians shipped 2,000 crates of potatoes. American and European church organizations pledged almost half a million dollars in food, medicines, and clothing to the CPRA relief operation.

While Graber rejoiced at these signs of progress, local developments threatened the future of his program. The contingent of Tunisian U.N. troops keeping the peace mandate in South Kasai was replaced with Ghanians. Ghana had aligned herself with Communist-bloc countries in defending Lumumba; Ghanian troops held Lumumba in custody in Leopoldville, protecting him from authorities of the Central Government and King Kalonji, who wanted to bring him to trial. The people of South Kasai had no basis for friendship with Ghanian troops.

Moreover, a battalion of Ghanian troops guarding the southern border of the province reported turning back a Belgian-led force of five thousand armed Baluba tribesmen attempting to invade the province and wrest its control from the U.N. peace-keeping forces. King Kalonji and three Belgian traders, including Swaenen who had befriended Graber at Mwena Ditu, were arrested for complicity. There were sporadic outbreaks of violence between the Ghanians and supporters of Kalonji, with an occasional killing. Ill will between the groups mounted to hair-trigger intensity. Rash threats and counter threats helped press the land to the brink of war. Kalonji's subsequent release helped curb the outbreak of widespread hostilities.

Finally, Graber read clues of growing disfavor of the South Kasai government toward his relief efforts. At that time CPRA was the only agency ministering to Baluba refugees. Graber's work was highly visible. First, the Kalonji government made its right to appoint distribution personnel a condition to paying their salaries. Graber kept his own workers, whom he knew to be trustworthy, and paid them from CPRA funds. Authorities said that his system of using family ration cards introduced discrimination into feeding operations; they required that he stop using them.

On November 14 the government demanded that CPRA signs be removed from its trucks; government property could not be utilized to promote a religious enterprise. Archie postponed the issue by asking that the request be put into writing so that it could be sent to Leopoldville and handled officially by his CPRA superiors. Such tactics suggested that the Kalonji government hoped to use the CPRA relief program as a means of strengthening its political support among the Baluba people.

Graber did not allow these ploys to reduce his efforts. Rather, he expanded them. He opened new feeding centers every week until they numbered twenty. His trucks were in the road every day, keeping the centers supplied. Periodically in his travels he would meet clusters of refugees from Charlesville or Tshikapa; he encouraged them to build chapels and begin worship.

In a social climate where many factors worked to compound human suffering, the CPRA worked to alleviate it. The organization's food curbed hunger; its clothing covered bodies; its medicines healed diseases; its tents offered shelter. Its reputation sped toward the far limits of the 7,500-square-mile famine-stricken area. Refugee Paul Badibanga, who grew up at Charlesville during the years Archie was there, spoke for many others when he later described the significance of Graber's ministry during those days:

"When Lutonga arrived, we felt like God had come to see us that day. Hunger surpassed us. We fought. We wrangled. We pushed. Lutonga would move in among us. He kept greeting us, restraining noise. telling us to stand in a nice row so that they could give us things. When we were quiet, he read a few verses to us from Exodus chapter 12. Then he would speak to us. 'Long ago Pharaoh drove the people of Israel into the wilderness,' he said. 'Sometimes they were hungry. Sometimes they were at war. But in their sufferings, God helped them. He led them across the wilderness to the River Jordan. Then Joshua, their leader, gathered them together and said, "Let's give ourselves to God to see if He will show us a way to get across this river so we can go into our land." God showed them a way. You've been driven into the wilderness. God brought you to this land. There are still some big rivers to cross. We've brought you these little things which might help you. We're all suffering together. Now let's all pray and give ourselves to God to see if He will show us a way to get across these rivers and bring an end to our suffering.' Then he prayed that the sick and weak would be healed and that the mourning would be comforted. He thanked God for the kind people across the great water who sent us these things, and asked God to bless these things to make us strong. Then he would leave distribution in the hands of his helpers and move on to another place. When war broke out at one place, he would move on to another. He never stopped working, so that we refugees might have a bit of rest.''

Paul Mukendi, son of Pastor Luaba, said, ''When Lutonga came to Miabi with tents, people rejoiced surpassingly. Those tents kept people from sleeping outside under the sky. He gave one to me for my family. We set it up, went inside of it, and sat down. I told my wife, 'Look how God is everywhere! Look how He is our caretaker! He rescued us from the fighting at Luluabourg. He protected us along the road where there was hunger and war. Then when many were killed in fighting here, we escaped. Now, from Lutonga we get the help of this tent that we weren't expecting!' So we poured our thanks out to God for His care to us.''

Archie was gratified with the progress. But his travels had acquainted him with need throughout the area. He knew his efforts were but a drop in the bucket. Economically, the province was impoverished. Diamond company officials loaned him use of a vacant residence. It had been looted, even to linens and kitchenware. Archie had great difficulty refurnishing it. There was virtually nothing to purchase in Bakwanga. He managed to trade some corn flour for a pan to use for boiling water; and in an African village sixty miles away, he found six bowls to use for coffee and soup.

It was clear to Graber that meeting the genuine need of 300,000 destitute refugees required two things: first, immediate availability of mass quantities of food to check the spread of famine, and second, a long-range rehabilitation effort until people were living in their own homes and eating produce from their own fields. How could a program of such scope ever be realized? Who were the qualified personnel to carry it out? Where would money for it come from?

Archie returned from a business trip to Leopoldville on November 24, Thanksgiving Day. News awaiting him seemed to confirm that the dream of an adequate relief program was pure illusion; the news even jeopardized the future of what little he was already doing.

"I found a letter from Prime Minister Ngalula," Graber wrote in his diary. "He refuses for the trucks to haul any more food until the CPRA insignia are taken off their doors. If it were not that these people are dying for want of food, I would turn these two trucks back and tell them to carry on as they wish. That letter left me feeling just a little blue. Then I opened an envelope from Fort Wayne, Indiana. It had a letter from Irma and a picture of Nancy and Fluffy. That letter and picture made Thanksgiving for me. I had no breakfast this morning. Now I just had a tin of pea soup. 'When ye do well, and suffer for it, ye take it patiently, this is acceptable with God' (1 Peter 2:20). We'll just praise the Lord anyhow."

For the next two days Graber and two local Presbyterian missionaries met with South Kasai President Kalonji, Prime Minister Ngalula, and Commissioner of Refugees Kalala. The officials' position was inflexible. They presented Graber with a two-page outline for a restructured program which would bring all relief efforts under government jurisdiction.

Graber insisted that his efforts serve to turn the eyes of needy people toward a heavenly Father who loved them and wanted to save them not only from their hunger, but from their sin. He refused to let the spiritual dimension of his work be lost in a purely humanitarian effort. He and the government could not reach agreement. One of the missionaries, Dr. Hugh Farrior, who had his own plane, was delegated to fly to Leopoldville to consult with CPRA authorities there in an effort to resolve the crisis.

19

... Manna From Heaven ...

ON NOVEMBER 27, 1960, the day Hugh Farrior arrived at Leopoldville to report the impasse between Graber and the South Kasai government, CPRA authorities were meeting with a team of four United Nations experts who had just returned from a trip to Bakwanga to explore the Baluba refugee problem. It was the team's consensus that only a crash program of food relief could stave off mass starvation. Minimal diet needs for the estimated 250,000 refugees would require forty-five tons of food per day. The large number of victims of advanced starvation required that food relief be administered by medical experts.

John Grun, a United Nations authority with experience in UNICEF,[1] went to Bakwanga to survey the situation, confirmed the finding of the team of experts, and demanded a large-scale relief program for South Kasai. His report was relayed to United Nations headquarters in New York City. U.N. General Secretary Dag Hammarskjold announced the plight of the Baluba refugees to the world and appealed for multinational aid to curb epidemic famine.

The U.N. Food and Agricultural Organization set up a six-million-dollar relief program to aid South Kasai and invited twenty-six countries to help. Journalists rushed to Bakwanga to see what was called "the world's worst famine in 20 years."[2] Their reports, submitted to the mass media, focused world attention on the plight of Congo's Baluba refugees.

While a score of nations organized machinery to ship food, agency

[1]United Nations International Children's Emergency Fund.
[2]"Harvest of Anarchy in the Congo," *Life,* 17 February 1961, p. 22.

heads meeting in Leopoldville, Congo, organized to distribute it. Relief efforts of all interested groups would be coordinated within the structure of the United Nations program. The U.N. would arrange with the Congo government for the tax-free importation of commodities, and would carry responsibility for transporting them inland to the famine-stricken area. All food would be pooled and stored in U.N. warehouse facilities.

Responsibilities for distribution were defined. The CPRA would supply foods and medicines to dispensaries and hospitals; the United Nations and CARITAS[3] would distribute food to refugees in villages. Ghanian troops and vehicles already on location would be utilized in the distribution. It was hoped that the greatly reduced visibility of Archie Graber's efforts within the context of the U.N. operation, along with the division of responsibilities, would reduce tensions.

During the interim, while top-echelon authorities consulted in Leopoldville to draw up a mutually agreeable plan for the expanded program of relief, Graber continued distributing food to the hungry. It did not occur to him that disagreement with the local government was sufficient cause to allow people to starve to death. During the week immediately following Farrior's flight to Leopoldville, Graber's government-loaned trucks clocked over a hundred miles a day to deliver supplies to feeding centers.

On December 4 Archie's longstanding request for the help of a veteran missionary was granted. Glenn Rocke arrived. Rocke had served at Charlesville for fifteen years, to 1960.[4] Now, loaned from AIMM to the South Kasai CPRA program, he had left his wife and four sons at Groveland, Illinois, and come to help.

On a living room wall of their residence, Graber and Rocke laid out a floor-to-ceiling map of the 60-by-120 mile famine-stricken area. It would help them keep track of their feeding centers; it would visually pinpoint for them areas of crucial need they discovered in their travels.

Graber wanted to encourage refugees to plant fields so that they could soon become self-supporting. He had distributed some seed corn; but as one father put it, "How can I plant corn my children are crying for?" The food staple of Central African peoples is cassava. Archie and Glenn took trucks into distant, less-affected areas to get the woody stems of the cassava plant. They bartered three bags of rice for a truckload, and

---

[3]The executive arm in Congo of the Catholic Relief Services, National Catholic Welfare Conference of the United States.
[4]See page 115.

distributed seven truckloads to the refugee villages. Even hungry people could not eat sticks. They planted them.

Meanwhile, in Leopoldville, John Grun was appointed Chief U.N. Refugee Coordinator. With the new agreement in hand, he and other U.N. officials flew to Bakwanga. On December 9 the U.N. team and South Kasai government authorities called a meeting with relief personnel to explain the new program. To Archie, utilization of the U.N. structure to rapidly import vast quantities of food was an answer to prayer beyond his dreams. Perhaps mass starvation would be avoided and the spread of famine checked. The program looked good on paper. He agreed to try to cooperate with it. But within himself, he had serious reservations about how it would work in practice.

It apparently went unrecognized that no one was more knowledgeable in the matter of feeding Baluba refugees than Graber. Because he was not consulted, he did not offer his opinion. But he knew well the covert conflicting social and political dynamics which the new program would have to cope with. CPRA was to confine its relief work to supplying hospitals and dispensaries, while the U.N. and CARITAS would minister to refugees in villages. Hospitals and dispensaries were located in villages. How could famine-stricken people be so neatly partitioned? How could ministering agencies making their best efforts to respect such partitioning remain above criticism? When friends he had made during his thirty years in Congo arrived at his home, distraught with grief, weakened by famine, could he deny them aid because they were not at a hospital?

What would it mean for CPRA to surrender its identity within the larger structure? He could not compromise his purpose; his efforts must witness for Jesus Christ. As an integral part of a gigantic humanitarian effort, would he be allowed to continue offering relief with a spiritual dimension, or were authorities hoping that his Christian witness would now be swallowed up and silenced? He kept relief food for which CPRA had already paid import duty and transport costs; he felt he should have the say about how it was to be used.

Meanwhile the CPRA team strengthened efforts to help hospitals and dispensaries. One aspect of this new program gave Archie special satisfaction. It enabled him to focus his attention on the sustained provision of food and medicines to innocent victims of famine whose suffering was most cruel — the thousands of children who had gravitated to medical centers with the dread protein-deficiency disease of kwashiorkor.

Some refugees were too weak to gather firewood to cook food for themselves or their children. Graber built crude stick-and-thatch kitchens and hired cooks. He would cut an empty, fifty-gallon fuel drum around its middle, cut air vents and a door hole for inserting firewood in each of the halves, and up-end them onto the ground to serve as stoves on which to cook food. At points where the sick were not receiving medicine, the CPRA team would either convert an available abandoned building into a medical dispensary or construct one of temporary materials. Then they would set up a feeding center.

The U.N. airlift of food directly to Bakwanga began during the third week of December. CPRA personnel helped haul commodities from the DC-6 cargo planes to the U.N. warehouse. Christmas was approaching. U.N. authorities had offered the CPRA team the generous gift of a free trip to Leopoldville. Graber was looking forward to going there for the holidays. On December 23 he was called to Bakwanga headquarters office of the U.N. relief operation. There he found Chief Coordinator Grun from Leopoldville and four other uniformed U.N. personnel.

"Mr. Graber, I want to introduce you to Mr. Xavier Caballero," Grun said, motioning toward one of the men. "He has been put in charge of U.N. operations in Bakwanga. As you know, planes are bringing in food every day. Stocks in the warehouse are mounting. It was our plan to use the Ghanian contingent of U.N. troops here to distribute food to the refugees. However, there seems to be an atmosphere of great suspicion here toward the Ghanians. Refugees will not take food from them. Due to some unfortunate incidents between the Ghanians and troops of President Kalonji, there is even the fear that a Ghanian convoy taking food into rural areas could be attacked. You have been here for some months. You know the African language. CPRA trucks are well known in the area. We are wondering if you would be willing to lead a convoy to a rural refugee area tomorrow to allay suspicions of people so that the distribution program can get under way."

Incredible! A six-million-dollar relief program to curb mass famine claimed world headlines. It had set machinery in motion in unnumbered distant lands. It had brought an international team of skilled specialists to the scene of distress. It had initiated a mercy airlift of cargo planes landing daily at Bakwanga to disgorge scores of tons of food. Now, at the final point of alleviating appalling suffering, the program had ground to a halt. The destined beneficiaries rejected it. And top-echelon U.N. officials were looking to Graber, an obscure bush missionary, to resolve the problem. Had God called him to help Baluba refugees in ways he had not anticipated? It was mind-boggling. Helping them out would put an end to his hopes of spending Christmas with friends in Leopoldville. But it need not affect plans for the rest of his team. The role the U.N. was asking him to play was too important to miss.

"Sure I'll go with you," he replied. "What time do you want to leave?"

Unwittingly, Graber was beginning to fill the role of an indispensable fix-it man whose tools were invisible, but unique.

They left about eight o'clock the following morning. The U.N. force of Ghanians would maintain low profile on this first trip to reduce the risk of open hostility. They would distribute food in villages west of Bakwanga in the direction of Lake Munkamba, along a road much traveled by CPRA vehicles. Three large trucks were loaded with relief food; a CPRA truck, a U.N. truck, and a Red Cross truck. Graber drove the CPRA truck and led the convoy; the U.N. truck with Ghanian distributors came second, and the Red Cross truck with medical personnel followed.

When they approached a refugee settlement, Graber would arrive some distance ahead of the second vehicle. He would stop the CPRA truck, quickly get out of the cab, stand full height on the running board, smile, wave, and shout a greeting. Then, as was his custom, he would begin shaking hands. By the time people were done greeting him, the U.N. truck had arrived and Ghanians were busy preparing to distribute food. The convoy traveled twenty miles, to the town of Kabeya Kamuanga, where a large number of Graber's friends from the AIMM field had relocated; after distributing food there, the trucks returned to Bakwanga without incident. From this beachhead the United Nations gradually extended its program of food distribution throughout the area.

It was quiet when Archie got home that evening. Everyone else had gone to Leopoldville. He was invited by diamond company officials to attend a Christmas Eve banquet at their downtown clubhouse. He cleaned up, dressed, and went.

It was a gala occasion. The long, rectangular hall was decorated with a large, imported evergreen tree draped with some tinsel, and a few large red paper bells suspended from the ceiling. The decorations clashed with the large African motifs painted on the walls, but they provided a festive air. The situation at Bakwanga at this time neither allowed nor required a large number of prominent persons; everybody who was anybody was there . . . a gathering of mutually acquainted notables.

Archie was shown to a place at one of the rectangular tables. On his one hand sat a U.N. nutritions expert; on his other sat the South Kasai government minister of health. He watched arriving guests — people representing the diamond mining company, the U.N., the government, the Catholic church. They all smiled politely, greeted each other, shook hands, and exchanged appropriate pleasantries. Graber marveled how Christmas had worked its magic effect; this evening, mixed elements which exploded on other days were rendered benign.

Drinks were served at 8:30 P.M. African drummers entertained. Then followed the meal: a plate of hor d'oeuvres; an entrée of fish and mushrooms; the main course of roasted turkey, peas, carrots, potatoes, and gravy. Courses were leisurely spaced. There was an occasional brief speech . . . a pianist who played Christmas carols . . . time for relaxed chit-chat. The experience was a pleasant change for Graber. But clearly, it was a facade.

What were the powerful, emotion-laden feelings that swirled just below the surface of this polite geniality? These were the persons whose conduct would determine the final outcome of his efforts under CPRA. What were the emotions shaping the separate roles these persons would play? Would this whole drama end in triumph or in tragedy?

Take President Kalonji, for example. His short and sinewy frame seemed relaxed at the table. His high forehead and smooth, fair complexion gave him a sleek look. His eyes were quick and sharp, his manner curt. His French was as impeccable as his dress. He was not a bad man; perhaps it was the cleverness essential to his survival which gave him something of the qualities of a fox. What complex, interwoven forces he must be coping with!

There was a threat from the west: the Congo Central Government, with headquarters in Leopoldville, hoped to topple him. There was a threat from the north: Antoine Gizenga had established headquarters at

Stanleyville and had proclaimed himself heir to the arrested Lumumba and rightful president of the Congo. Pro-Communist nations were shipping him arms, and his troops were making adventuresome forays in the direction of South Kasai.

There was a threat from within. Kalonji's title "King of the Baluba" was of declaration, not of right. Traditionally, the progenitor of the Baluba peoples had two sons, and the right of chieftainship followed the line of his firstborn. Kalonji was a descendant of the secondborn.

Unquestionably, the primary factor that would determine Kalonji's attitude toward agencies and personnel around him was political survival . . . he would take the position that would enhance the possibility of his continuing in power. He would be alert to lay hold upon anything which would strengthen his position, and quick to eliminate anything which threatened it. To what extremes might this attitude force him?

This explained his shift in attitude toward the ministry of CPRA. At first he had sought out agency authorities in Leopoldville to thank them for their help; he had chartered planes to fly CPRA relief commodities to Bakwanga. Now he seemed to be suspicious of its growing popularity with the people; he had sent it a bill for $600,000 for transportation costs; increasingly he insisted that CPRA efforts be brought under government control. What were his inner feelings about the newly expanded relief program? Would he uncomplainingly allow the United Nations to play the role of great benefactor to his people?

The modicum of allegiance he gave the Central Government to keep peace with it did not allow him to show undue friendship toward Belgians. Still, diamond revenue was essential to his political survival. This helped explain his on-again off-again relationships with Belgian diamond mine management . . . relationships which this banquet had been designed to improve.

The descendant of the firstborn and rightful heir to the chieftainship of the Baluba people was Prime Minister Ngalula, second in power to Kalonji. He was of medium height and stocky build; his face was almost pudgy. He seemed friendly, approachable, diplomatic. How long would he and his people be content in a position subordinate to Kalonji and his clan? The Kalonji-Ngalula alliance was at best tenuous.

The minister of health seated next to Archie had frequently been helpful in pointing out ways CPRA could fit into the program. Then there was the Catholic bishop, Monsignor Nkongolo. His thinking did not necessarily reflect that of the Catholic church. He had announced in public meetings that there was to be only one church in the Baluba Kingdom, and he was its priest. He nurtured friendship with government authorities to that end. Finally, the commissioner of refugees, Kalala, had shown little sympathetic interest in the work of CPRA. In all probability, he was ready to serve the interests of either Bishop Nkongolo or the Kalonji government.

Dignitaries present that night represented a maelstrom of powerful, shifting, swirling eddies. It appeared that CPRA was a little stick caught in the midst of them, tossing, bobbing, perhaps one day to be sucked under forever. About eleven o'clock, toward the end of the evening's program, table waiters brought from the kitchen a brown cake about four feet long and a foot wide. It was a simulated Yule Log. On it large green letters spelled out in French, "Joyous Christmas!" There were exclamations of delight. The cake was pretty. But somehow Graber wished the joy were not so hollow.

Following Christmas the U.N. relief program rapidly picked up momentum. The airlift peaked in January 1961, when cargo planes arrived one every twenty minutes and unloaded ninety tons of food per day. Some thirty white U.N. trucks shuttled food to 180 distribution points, which fed 200,000 refugees daily.

CPRA personnel continued transporting supplies to medical feeding centers. During January they hauled 226 tons of food to sixty-four dispensaries and six hospitals. Frequently a loaded truck would perilously escape capsizing a ferry, or would bog down in sand or mud and keep workers in the road overnight. Where larger quantities of cooked food were required, Archie would cut a fifty-gallon drum in two, and use each of the halves as a huge cooking pot on an open fire. He continued to build temporary kitchens and medical dispensing shelters from poles, sticks, and grass.

Joint relief efforts under the U.N. curbed the spread of famine. By the end of January, world wire services reported that the dead and dying no longer lay by the roadsides. Daily death rate had been reduced from over two hundred to perhaps forty or fifty, and the limbs of small children were beginning to flesh out again.[5]

[5] "Worst Period Surmounted by U.N. Relief," *London Times,* 27 January 1961, p. 12.

Bringing famine under control was a monumental achievement. But efforts could not be relaxed. The forty-five-ton daily flow of food must continue until the refugees could support themselves with produce from their own fields. Frequently Archie would catch a flight on a U.N. plane headed for Leopoldville to buy more supplies.

Now that famine was checked, he anticipated the day when he could relate his efforts more directly to the work of the church. Now, while in the capital city, he arranged for the printing of 50,000 Gospels of John and ordered 1,000 Bibles in the African language. He purchased a new Volkswagen minibus to convert into a bookmobile for literature distribution.

His October order for transport trucks had never materialized. Now he bought a five-ton Mercedes truck, tried to expedite its shipment, and ordered a second one. He visited the U.S. Embassy and ordered six thousand tons of American corn flour. He purchased corrugated sheet roof metal and nails sufficient to build twenty-five kitchens; these materials he needed immediately. He went to Coordinator Grun's office for help.

"When it's raining and cold outside, the women won't come to cook," he explained. "Those refugees must eat every day. You assigned us the job of feeding these people at hospitals and dispensaries. If you want us to do the job, you've got to see that these things get there."

Grun arranged to ship the eight tons of materials by air directly to Bakwanga.

Archie's presence continued to prove important to the U.N. program. Health officials decided that use of a helicopter would help them to quickly determine medical needs in isolated villages. They asked Graber to join them on the first flight. By this time his use of the large wall map had made him well acquainted with the location of villages throughout the area. Three U.N. personnel — a pilot, co-pilot, and doctor — and Graber, all whites, made up the team. Advance word of their coming had been sent to the villages.

They landed at the first village on their itinerary. Graber served as interpreter. They completed the survey successfully. Then they flew into a more remote area and located the second village. It was set on the crest of a hill. They circled it, hunting for a landing place, and decided to set the craft down on the hillside about two hundred yards below the village.

"As soon as we touch down," the doctor shouted to Graber, "you head for the village. Tell them who we are and what we've come for."

On touch-down Archie jumped from the craft and started up the hill. He met two village men approaching the landing site and introduced himself. Word sent in advance had not arrived. Graber and the two men proceeded up the hill to explain what was happening. When they reached a point about fifty yards from the village, an outbreak of angry shouts from the rear arrested him. Graber turned to look.

The pilot, co-pilot, and doctor were standing by the copter, their hands back of their heads, surrounded by a dozen of Kalonji's soldiers shouting and pointing guns at them.

"Wait!" Graber yelled. "Let me explain!"

The soldiers were irrational with frenzy. This big bird suddenly dropping out of the sky must be the white man's clever way of launching a surprise military attack; Kalonji's soldiers were threatening to eliminate the invaders. Graber's shouting was pointless. He well knew that a suspicious move by any one of them meant instant death.

"Wait! Don't shoot!" the two Africans accompanying Archie called as they broke into a run down the hill. Remaining behind them, Archie cautiously approached the scene.

"These whites have not come to do us evil," one of them explained. "This is Preacher Lutonga, the man who passes back and forth along these roads in the CPRA truck feeding our refugees."

"My friends, we did not mean to scare you," Graber spoke in their language. "We sent word ahead, but it did not arrive. We do not have it in our hearts to harm a one of you. We came to see if there are sick and hungry among you. We want to help them."

The soldiers grumbled until their frustrations were vented, then lowered their guns. The team completed its survey and left. It was clear that the U.N. men owed their lives to the presence of Graber. They abandoned the rest of the itinerary and returned to Bakwanga. Graber requested that the U.N. not use the helicopter in this type of survey. It frightened the people too much; its use was fraught with danger. That was their last such trip.

CPRA continued to make its contribution under the canopy of the U.N., but with some difficulty. In fact, from early January Graber sensed they were sailing into a storm.

During the late evening hours of January 5, Cabellaro, director of

Glenn Rocke collects "Tshombe sticks," cuttings of the manioc. *(MCC)*

Cooking on a fuel-drum stove; Robert Bontrager (second from left), CPRA chairman, looks on. *(AIMM)*

Archie with bookmobile *(AIMM)*

Lumberyard to provide shelter and employment for refugees

Archie Graber, Glenn Rocke, and a Congolese inspecting new shoots of corn, which promise hope for a coming harvest and food for a hungry people *(AIMM)*

Archie handing out chicks to Congolese *(MCC)*

U.N. operations in South Kasai, visited Graber. "Bishop Nkongolo will no longer allow a Protestant organization to deliver food to Catholic institutions; he demands that the Catholic church share in the work of distributing food to hospitals and dispensaries. A chief point of contention is the CPRA signs you continue to display on trucks loaned you by the government. The feeling is that a humanitarian cause should not be used to propagate religion. Rather than provoke a crisis which might disrupt the feeding program, we urge you to remove the signs from the government trucks."

On the following morning Graber complied; but he left the insignia on his CPRA–owned Volkswagen minibus. Within a few weeks, the South Kasai government demanded the return of both its trucks. The two Mercedes trucks Graber had ordered for CPRA work in South Kasai arrived to replace them. He praised the Lord for bringing them at precisely the right time. Inasmuch as they were property of the agency he represented, he painted the CPRA signs on their doors. He felt the signs were important not only to identify his relief work with the cause of Christ and the church but also for his personal safety. Trigger-happy tribal vigilante groups would be much less likely to attack a CPRA truck than an unmarked one.

On January 17 Caballero told Graber that observers of CPRA feeding procedures had reported to Bishop Nkongolo that Graber told people the food he distributed had come from friends in America, and that he prayed with them before he left. Caballero did not object to Graber's praying, but urged him to avoid mentioning the name of America; even U.N. authorities were beginning to yield to growing insistence of the Kalonji government to take over all distribution of commodities so that the Baluba people would recognize it alone as their benefactor.

Kalonji was compelled to muster all available support for his administration. Mounting political pressures threatened his survival. Kwame Nkrumah, then president of Ghana, joined Communist-bloc nations in announcing support of Lumumba-heir Gizenga in Stanleyville as the rightful president of Congo. This support of Kalonji's archenemy further poisoned relations between his government and the U.N. Ghanian troops assigned to keep the peace in South Kasai. Forays of Gizenga's troops were approaching South Kasai borders. Kalonji initiated military training after work hours for all adult males; he put his army on alert against invasion by Gizenga's troops, who could quickly join forces with the Ghanians to topple him. He issued a decree forbidding the Baluba to fraternize with Ghanians under penalty of a stiff fine and two months in jail. Six political prisoners were beheaded. Ghanian and Baluba troops clashed at Lake Munkamba, leaving a Kalonji soldier dead.

Meanwhile, decisions were made in Washington, D.C., which aggravated the problem. In early February President Kennedy announced the position of the U.S. government toward the Congo political crisis. To discourage the further balkanization of Congo into hostile tribal states, all Congolese were to be disarmed; peace-keeping was to be entrusted to U.N. forces. Belgians were to be expelled, and Lumumba was to be released to participate in the formation of a broad coalition government.

Such a proposal was anathema to the Baluba. America, home of their Protestant missionaries, had betrayed them. It had taken sides with their enemies. American citizens in their midst could be suspected of complicity with the Ghanians for the overthrow of the South Kasai Free State. Missionaries were arrested. Their transmitters were seized. Mission planes were grounded; their airstrips were closed. Two top Belgian mine executives and Archie's Baluba mechanic were imprisoned for fraternizing with Ghanians. Graber and Rocke stopped preaching at weekly Ghanian worship services.

In early February the Kalonji government demanded that all relief work be coordinated under its commissioner of refugees. In a series of long and painful sessions with the commissioner during following weeks, the screws were tightened on the ministry of CPRA.

Graber was compelled to remove CPRA signs from the agency's vehicles. The commissioner refused to authorize lists of commodities Graber proposed distributing to hospitals and dispensaries. In a report prepared by the government on the quantities of foodstuffs distributed by relief agencies, CPRA, while having distributed more than any of the others, was not mentioned.[6] One day the commissioner crossed out a full-page list of food Graber proposed distributing and angrily announced, "The CPRA no longer exists."

Complaints intensified against the two young Americans driving

---

[6]The report, covering the period December 14 to February 2, was as follows: United Nations: 423 tons; South Kasai government: 209 tons; diamond mine company: 35 tons; CPRA: 526 tons; Red Cross: unspecified quantity of milk.

CPRA trucks. They occupied two places of employment which should be held by Baluba wage earners. Their knowing neither French nor the native language had been a basis for growing misunderstanding. Now, with anti-American feeling running high, they could be shot at the drop of a hat. Archie packed them onto a U.N. plane headed for Leopoldville. That left Graber alone with Rocke. Their work: building kitchens.

"Things are getting pretty rough around here," Archie wrote home in mid-February. "The U.N. is finding it more and more difficult to carry on its feeding program. Swiss Red Cross officials have asked that no more food be shipped them until further notice; they may be leaving. Some thirty Austrian doctors are finding it most difficult to carry on. Ghanian soldiers are like poison, missionaries are on edge, and it looks like the work of CPRA is about finished."

20

... Up From Ashes ...

THESE WERE DISCOURAGING days for Graber and Rocke. Why should they stay any longer if they weren't wanted? Maybe they should simply pack up and leave. There was one important fact which made such a course impossible. They knew that decrees of the incumbent government did not reflect feelings of the Baluba people at large; and the Baluba people demonstrated a spirit so indomitable that it seemed no measure of discouragement could extinguish it.

Graber recalled what he recently had seen in a town once completely destroyed by fire. In front of a CPRA tent-home someone had planted a canna. It was blooming. One day when traveling through a once famine-stricken area, he encountered a freshly built chapel set in greening village gardens. It was packed with refugees lustily singing, "Draw me nearer . . . nearer, blessed Lord. . . ." On another occasion a veteran Bible school teacher who had lost his home, his possessions, and a daughter in the fires of tribal warfare, chose as his sermon text, "I want you to understand, brethren, that the things which have happened to me have turned out for the furtherance of the gospel" (Phil. 1:12).

This spirit of courage, of ambition, of personal worth . . . from where did they get it? Something of what Archie had helped them discover within themselves two decades earlier was remanifesting itself here; now it was reciprocating its benefits to him. He simply could not abandon them and betray that kind of spirit. Such signs helped confirm for the two men that God had called them there and that their ministry was not yet finished.

The tense anti-foreigner climate required that they maintain a low profile. Almost daily they received appeals for food from medical centers whose supplies were exhausted — appeals to which they were powerless to respond. Quietly they did what they could. They built kitchens and a medical dispensary. No one disturbed them, except in frontier areas where they were occasionally stopped and examined by edgy Kalonji troops scouting for pro-Lumumba invaders. About two weeks passed. Then, on February 27, much to their surprise, they were called to the office of Prime Minister Ngalula.

"You are well acquainted with the region, and you know our people," the prime minister said. "Every plane landing here is loaded with refugees. We would like for you to find locations in the countryside where refugees can become established. Then you can transport refugees to these locations so that they can start building their own homes and planting their own gardens."

Graber praised the Lord. Just as he had suspected, some authorities in government were pulling for him. Not only was the government again recognizing CPRA as an existing agency, but it was inviting CPRA to make a contribution for which it was uniquely fitted — village planting. Unwittingly, it was opening the door for Graber to enter the second level of ministry which he had long envisioned — rehabilitation.

Arriving refugees were congesting at two transit camps on the outskirts of the city. The tents donated by German churches again proved invaluable. Archie and Glenn distributed them among camp refugees to provide temporary shelter. Then the two men roamed the countryside, hunting settlement sites. Consulting with rural government officials and village chiefs, they located roadside areas with good soil and water nearby.

Back at the city, they would load each CPRA truck with ten tents, some food, and about thirty-five refugees from a transit camp. Then they would drive to a resettlement location, unload the refugees, and help them erect an instant tent village. They distributed food and Christian literature among them. When necessary, they provided seed for planting and hoes for cultivating. They tried to see that each refugee village group included at least one committed Christian family which could serve as a nucleus for village worship, and whose head could serve as lay pastor.

Graber was a man who had to make things move. His instructions were curt. "Hurry and make yourselves simple houses for shelter," he would say."In a few weeks we'll return to get these tents for other people to use elsewhere. Make your gardens. We'll try to bring you some food until you are raising your own. When Sunday comes, remember to gather yourselves together and worship God. The refugees are so many; we can help you for only a short time. So get to work."

After prayer, the missionaries would leave.

The Baluba have the proverb, "If you don't use your hoe to make a field, someone else will use it to make your grave." They understood their crisis. They understood Lutonga. So they got to work. For several weeks the CPRA trucks were a familiar sight, crisscrossing the dusty roads of South Kasai with their bouncing loads of refugees. The transit camps were emptied. Then the pace of the program was reduced to handle the inflow of refugees upon their arrival.

South Kasai terrain is mostly gently rolling, treeless grassland. Refugees had difficulty finding poles and sticks with which to build their huts. At the same time, a large number of them had sold personal effects before emigrating; they arrived with money in their pockets. Building materials were not available to buy. Archie conceived the idea of establishing a retail building-supplies depot to offer, at prices barely above cost, materials essential for building their houses. This would also make it possible for him to provide remunerative employment to heads of families hired to handle the materials.

He stocked raw lumber, nails, hinges, carpentry tools, sheet-metal roofing, cement for pouring floor slabs, whitewash for dressing walls. Soon the enterprise was expanding into a small industry. He hired carpenters to prefabricate roof trusses, casements with fitted doors, window frames with fitted shutters, and to make scores of boxes for hand-pressing adobe brick. He bought hand-operated, cement-block-making machines, and employed eight men to make blocks for sale. The total operation was run largely by Africans and was self-supporting. By mid-May sales were running at nine hundred dollars a day.

Refugees demanded furniture. He hired more carpenters and made simple bedframes, tables, and chairs. September, the beginning of the school year, was less than six months away, and refugee children needed places to study. Funds were available from the government, from refugee donations, and from the CPRA budget. Workmen loaded CPRA trucks with cement blocks, ready-made trusses, and sheet-metal roofing, and erected school buildings. Carpenters built school desks by the hundreds.

Graber's primary problem was finding sources from which he could obtain adequate quantities of supplies. On April 4 he ordered 30 cement-block-making forms (promising employment for one hundred men) and 120 tons of cement. On June 17 in Elisabethville, the capital city of Tshombe's seceded province of Katanga, he bought 3 tons of nails and 16,000 sheets of corrugated roofing. In Leopoldville during the first week of July he purchased 2 tons of Bibles and Scripture portions, 3 tons of school supplies, and half a ton of carpenter hand tools. He chartered a plane which transported it all directly to Bakwanga. On July 27 in Luluabourg he arranged for shipping 40 tons of building materials by rail to Mwena Ditu.

On March 13, while on tour with four dignitaries from Washington, D.C., Archie scrounged the countryside to find a chicken, which he purchased for eight dollars and had cooked for their village meal. The experience prodded him to explore the possibility of importing baby chicks to supplement the meager refugee diet. His plan was to raise the chicks to about four weeks of age, and then sell them with a basic quantity of ready-mixed chicken feed to the Africans. If the need arose, his carpenters could prefabricate simple chicken hutches.

He ordered 500 baby chicks and feed from Elisabethville and launched the experiment. Response of the Africans was overwhelming. He ordered another 120 sacks of chicken feed and contacted CPRA officials in Leopoldville about arranging for an experimental shipment of baby chicks from the States. On June 29 a shipment of 1,000 day-old chicks from Sunnybrook Poultry Farms, Hudson, New York, arrived by regular commercial flight at Bakwanga. When workers removed chicks from their boxes, they counted 1,035; not one was found dead.

Pastor Kalala Kamburu, a refugee from Tshikapa, said, "Families were eating only cassava mush and greens; when company came, we felt shame; there was not the tiniest bit of meat to offer them. Then Lutonga started getting baby chicks. When they were a few months old, we would put about a hundred chickens in the minibus and go out to sell them. We sold them for $1.20 each. That was a ridiculous price. People fought over them. People coming to buy them were so many they couldn't find the man who was selling them. We would sell them all and then go get another hundred. Soon people began keeping roosters so they could hatch their own good chicks. This work helped everybody.''

Graber's efforts were not without problems. But he praised the Lord for signs of progress. The land was absorbing the present inflow of refugees. Almost everyone was busy building homes, schools, or chapels. To speed up the seeding of new fields, Graber later ordered two tractors from Leopoldville; they would be used to plow land adjacent to the new settlement areas. When political conditions made U.N. pilots balk at flying the tractors into Bakwanga, Archie wrote a telegram in English over the signature of a government minister guaranteeing the pilots' safety.

Suffering from hunger had once been most intense along the first twenty-five miles of road leading east from the tribal frontier at Lake Munkamba. Many had died along that roadside. Graber and his team had distributed scores of tons of food and truckloads of cassava plant cuttings there. Now the graves were largely forgotten. Teeming towns had sprung up along the road; they were linked by parallel green bands of waist-high cassava and tasseling corn.

The assignment of relocating refugees brought Archie back into close touch with the people again. Sometimes the stream of need was so continuous and so overwhelming that he longed to flee from it all. Then again an opportunity to help someone proved so fulfilling that he felt more than recompensed for the load he carried.

Joshua Kafuna had been a faithful mission teacher in a village of the Charlesville region from Archie's early years there. Kafuna took part in the church renovation program of 1939. In the post-independence events he lost everything and was driven to South Kasai. He settled with a large number of other AIMM Christians twenty miles west of Bakwanga at the town of Kabeya Kamuanga. An old man now, he resolved to do one last thing in his life. Before people had recovered from the weakness of famine, he began stirring them up.

''We're going to build a church,'' he announced. ''Not one of mud and stick. We've seen that kind fall down too many times. This one is going to be of concrete, so it lasts forever. Long ago Nehemiah said, 'Let's get together and build this wall.' For what reason can't we work together and build a church?''

Even the man's Bible text was reminiscent of 1939. Once when Archie and Glenn came to the town, Kafuna shared his vision.

''Preacher Lutonga, we want to build a church. It will be a memorial to the way God helped up through all our troubles. I've found stones for the foundation in the hillside a mile from here. We could carry them here on our heads; but people's bodies are not yet strong, and it would take a long time."

"You dig out the stones and put them on a pile," Lutonga replied. "Then whenever the CPRA truck comes and unloads its supplies, have the driver haul up a load of stone before he returns."

"Fine, preacher. As you know, almost all of us lost everything in the fighting. We will need cement blocks and roofing. Can you help us gather money to buy these things?"

Archie pondered a moment.

"All those village people who are in the CPRA truck when it comes back to Bakwanga, do they pay for their rides? Why should we carry them for nothing? When someone comes wanting a ride to Bakwanga, charge him thirty cents. When a woman comes with a big basin of cassava to take to Bakwanga to sell, charge her forty cents. Save that money. Add to it money from offerings Christians give. That's the way you'll build your church. Where are you going to build it?"

Kafuna showed the two missionaries the site. They stepped off the building's dimensions and knelt to pound in temporary corner stakes.

"Preachers with me, while you are here, we want to sanctify this place to God," the old man said.

He led them in prayer.

Archie had too many other things on his mind to think much more about the incident, until one day several months later when Kafuna arrived at Bakwanga. He gave Archie the money he had gathered — over $2,500. Archie loaded his trucks with cement blocks, truss lumber, and roofing and sent them to Kabeya Kamuanga. That's the way they built their church. The old man died a few years later. But the tall, simple-lined, memorial church still stands on the eastern edge of town, overlooking the broad, flat valley of the Lubi River.

Whatever anyone did those days was done in a climate of tension and uncertainty. Politics were still stormy and unpredictable, and Archie's efforts could never escape the incessant buffeting of their winds.

21

... 'Twill Be Better Further On ...

LUMUMBA'S MYSTERIOUS death in Katanga in mid-February of 1961 temporarily heightened tensions in South Kasai but caused no noticeable remorse. Government leaders occupied themselves with more pressing concerns. President Kasavubu of the Congo Central Government, Tshombe of Katanga, and Kalonji of South Kasai shared a mounting animosity toward the United Nations' peace-keeping force for what they felt was its interference in their states' internal affairs. The three of them also faced the common threat of advancing pro-Lumumba troops from the separatist Gizenga government headquartered in the northern city of Stanleyville. These shared concerns forced them to subdue their differences and stitch together some kind of political agreement whereby they could eliminate the threat of a Gizenga pro-Communist takeover and prove to the world that the United Nations' presence in Congo was unnecessary.

It was a fragile alliance. When heads of the three powers met in Madagascar in early March, Tshombe pressed through his resolution that Congo be a loose federation of separate sovereign states with a joint military council. Kalonji recognized that the winds were blowing favorably for him to confirm the political autonomy of his Baluba kingdom. He returned home, purportedly distributed gifts to clan chiefs to broaden his support base among the population, had himself publicly crowned king of the Baluba peoples, and accepted the accolade of his admirers.

"Seeing that you are the one who expelled the Belgian colonialists

187

from among us,'' they purportedly swore, ''there is no one who will ever take your place. You are the chief of all chiefs, as will be your offspring of each succeeding generation, one hooked onto the next, forever and ever.'' Supporters of Prime Minister Ngalula, descendants of the tribal father's firstborn, rumbled with discontent. The Central Government, in response to Kalonji's coronation, clamped a boycott on sales of all goods to South Kasai.

A follow-up conference to implement the Madagascar resolution was held in late April in the northeastern city of Coquilhatville, where the Central Government was sovereign. There President Kasavubu shifted his position to support the U.N. proposal for a strong central government. Tshombe saw this move as betrayal and refused to cooperate. Kasavubu had him arrested. Kalonji, to escape similar fate, broke with Tshombe and aligned with the Central Government. Kasavubu looked upon Kalonji's sudden pledge of allegiance with a suspicious eye and imposed strict control on importation of goods into South Kasai pending some proof of Kalonji's loyalty.

Agencies working in the country bore the repercussions of these events. Graber and Rocke were abruptly reminded of growing antagonism toward the U.N. when in late March they went to Luluabourg for supplies. They purchased blankets, medicated soap, Bibles, and foodstuffs, and loaded their trucks. They took their position in the middle of a twelve-truck U.N. convoy and began the ninety-mile trip home. Just after they crossed the tribal frontier into South Kasai at Lake Munkamba, Kalonji troops stopped the caravan at the roadblock. U.N. soldiers with guns in hand leaped from the front truck. The Kalonji troops faded into the high grass. The roadblock was dismantled, and the caravan proceeded.

Archie learned that his new Volkswagen minibus and other commodities shipped from Leopoldville had arrived by rail at Luluabourg and were held up there because of the anti-Kalonji embargo. His order of 50,000 Gospels had already arrived at Bakwanga, and he now had a good supply of Bibles on hand. He wanted to launch a bookmobile ministry with the new minibus. On Friday, April 28, he and Rocke flew to Luluabourg to see what they could do to expedite shipment of their goods.

They were buying supplies in a Belgian-operated store that afternoon, when suddenly there was a commotion across the plaza in front of the railroad station. People were running. Central Government army jeeps and U.N. jeeps, loaded with armed soldiers, began speeding down the streets. Storekeepers closed their doors. People vacated the streets and hurried home.

Some weeks earlier Central Government army troops had driven U.N. Syrian troops out of the west-coast port city of Matadi. Now word had just arrived that Central Government troops had massacred U.N. Ghanian soldiers at the city of Port Francqui, a river-rail junction 240 miles northwest of Luluabourg; twenty-eight bodies had been recovered from the river. News of the incident triggered a confrontation between U.N. and Congo army troops in Luluabourg that sped to the brink of violence. Archie and Glenn, along with everyone else, sat out the remaining tension-freighted hours of the day in quiet seclusion.

For two days the men tried unsuccessfully to clear permission to ship the goods. They did secure possession of the minibus. Then news reached them of trouble along the tribal frontier near Lake Munkamba. Should they drive the vehicle through to Bakwanga, or would they get caught in the middle of tribal warfare? They laid the matter out before the Lord in prayer.

"Dear Father," Archie prayed, "we would like to put this minibus on the road so that people can have Your Word. If Your Holy Spirit could tell the apostle Paul where to go and where not to go when he was on his missionary journeys, surely He can tell us whether or not we should go on this trip tomorrow." After prayer both Graber and Rocke felt prompted to make the trip. Also, they laid out a prayer fleece and were directed to go.

About ten o'clock the following morning, May 4, they started out. Rocke was driving. They had traveled eastward about twenty-five miles when they began noticing men walking along the roadside, armed with every kind of primitive weapon, also going east. As the missionaries pressed on, the number of armed men increased. The heads of some were bound with palm-frond battle wreaths; the bodies of others were marked with whitewash. Apparently every able-bodied male, from adolescent to aged, was answering some call to war. When the missionaries reached a certain village, they saw the road ahead of them teeming black with warriors. As Graber's eyes took in the scene, he sent a prayer heavenward: "Father, we believe Your Spirit told us to make this trip. Now surely You'll make a way for us to get through this mob of angry people.''

"We're in for a hard time here," he said to Rocke uneasily.

Rocke honked the horn. The mob held its ground, shouted angrily, brandished its weapons. Rocke braked the vehicle to a stop. Graber got out, reached in through a side door for a handful of Gospels, and began giving them out. The crowd surged forward, threatening to pin him against the vehicle. He threw the remaining booklets over their heads. The pressure eased, allowing him to reach for more. He heaved them over the heads toward the rear of the car. Some of the mob began pushing in the direction of the Gospels. Graber slipped back into the front seat and slammed the door. Rocke raced the motor and nudged the car forward. The phalanx of warriors before them began to break, and Rocke pressed the vehicle through them. They yelled protestingly as the bus broke free and sped on its way. In Archie's heart a hymn was ringing: "God leads His dear children along. . . ."

Then the missionaries noticed that almost immediately the landscape was deserted. Their sudden aloneness left them feeling uneasy. Gradually they understood. The village they had just passed through was the staging area for battle. Now they were passing through no man's land between the lines. What would they find waiting ahead?

At the tribal border line at Lake Munkamba the road was blocked with a heavy pole. Armed Kalonji soldiers in charge of the roadblock took Graber and Rocke half a mile down a side road toward the lake to a temporary military headquarters. A gruff commanding officer grilled them with questions: "Who are you?" "Where are you from?" "What are you doing?" "Why did you come at this time?" The missionaries answered the questions, volunteered no information about the assembled warriors, distributed Gospels to everyone present, gave a Bible to the Commanding officer, and were released. They resumed their journey. Several miles ahead, when they were clearly out of trouble, Archie spoke:

"Let's pull off the road here so we can thank the Lord we got through that place. Why don't you pray?"

Rocke stopped the minibus on the side of the road and led them in prayer:

"Our Father in heaven, we thank You that You brought us through that mob of people. We don't know what they are so angry about, but we pray that some of the Scriptures we left them will quiet them down so that there won't be so much bloodshed. And when they read the Word, may some of them be convicted of their sins and come to know Christ. We pray in His name. Amen.''

A few days after they arrived home, news reached them that the large Baluba village just inside the frontier at Lake Munkamba had been attacked and completely destroyed by fire. The attack, which occurred in the late hours of a morning when most people were away working in their fields, apparently had caught the Kalonji soldiers at the roadblock unawares. Archie recalled how these people had suffered in famine, and how they had struggled to build themselves shelters and to till new gardens. CPRA trucks had delivered scores of tons of food to this area. Just two weeks before, Archie had been there and prayed in the home of Kabodi, a friend from his years at Tshikapa. The man had heart trouble and was confined to his bed.

Now Graber and Rocke loaded a truck with tents and food and drove to the site of the devastated village.

The men found villagers stirring around in the ashes and rubble of their homes. After speaking some words to encourage them, Archie recalled his friend.

''Is Kabodi still here?''

''He had remained in his house because of his illness,'' village people explained. ''When warriors arrived, we were away in our fields. When they set our houses on fire, there was no one to help him. He burned to death.''

Over following weeks the two missionaries helped reestablish the people of the village. Graber and his helpers erected a six-room, cement-block school building in which refugees could live until they rebuilt their shelters. When the CPRA men arrived to begin constructing the building, they learned that Baluba soldiers had killed fifty-six enemy tribesmen along the lakefront the day before in an apparent retaliatory attack.

Heightening conflict between authorities of the Kalonji government and of the United Nations in South Kasai brought the two groups to a stalemate. Women working under the auspices of the U.N. left. Then the forty members of a U.N. Austrian medical staff left. Then Red Cross representatives left. One morning Graber learned that the entire contingent of the U.N. Ghanian troops with their vehicles and equipment had slipped out during the night. They felt their numbers were inadequate to successfully resist a surprise attack by Kalonji troops; they didn't want to be sitting ducks for another Port Francqui–style massacre.

Graber's immediate concern was how the departure of all U.N. personnel would affect the program of feeding refugees. The food airlift had been gradually replaced by food brought in by truck convoys from Luluabourg; shipping peaked at forty truckloads per day. Then recurring tribal warfare along the Lulua–Baluba frontier slowly strangled this avenue of entry. Next, it was planned to ship food by rail to Mwena Ditu, where U.N. trucks could load it for distribution.

This was a most inopportune time for the breakdown of the feeding program. Baluba people were affected by repercussions of the stormy, mid-April, three-power conference in Coquilhatville. When Kalonji aligned himself with the Central Government, whose troops had arrested Katangan president Tshombe, enmity was spawned toward Baluba residing in the province of Katanga. Few of them could escape to South Kasai; instead, by the thousands they fled for refuge in a U.N.–protected camp for political refugees on the outskirts of the Katangan capital of Elisabethville.

Events of the Coquilhatville conference heightened anti-Baluba sentiment throughout the country and sent fresh waves of refugees flooding into South Kasai. They were just beginning to arrive in mid-May when the U.N. feeding program broke down. By early July commercial flights to South Kasai were booked solid for two weeks in advance by refugees seeking asylum. The total number of immigrants into South Kasai by that time approached 500,000, boosting population density of the tiny province from 6 to 50 per square mile. Would a society just rising from the ruins of famine and war be able to absorb this new influx of refugees, or would its meager resources be exhausted, causing famine to break out again? Graber learned that the U.N. had sold the Kalonji government twelve trucks for it to use in carrying out the feeding program for which the U.N. once used sixty; he had serious doubts that such an arrangement would prove adequate.

On July 8 Archie heard that Baluba were being driven out of Lusambo, a city about 145 miles northeast of Bakwanga. There was no air transport available, so many refugees were headed for South Kasai on foot. He and two visitors loaded three cases of powdered milk into the old minibus and went to explore the situation.

The road was bad. It had been neglected since political independence a year before. Graber negotiated washouts which all but overturned the vehicle. Within a distance of thirty-five miles, they counted over five hundred refugees walking toward Bakwanga. Fresh graves dotted the roadside. The corpse of a woman was left abandoned, stripped naked; someone else needed her clothing. Graber and his guests gave a small package of milk powder to each of those who seemed to need it most; they returned heartsick that their supply had been but a paltry gesture in the face of such a need.

Signs of famine began to crop up in the city. One began seeing again a cluster of people sitting on the ground beside someone dead from hunger, or an emaciated person staring blankly into space. Refugees were accumulating in the transit camps again; the number of tents Graber loaned them for shelter climbed to two hundred. Occasionally there were beatings or shootings, when desperate men vented their passions.

Among refugees arriving at Bakwanga in mid-July were Pastor Matthew Kazadi, his wife, and his son from Charlesville. Archie saw the strange car arrive. When he recognized those who got out of it, he was at first stupefied and then profoundly grateful; rumors that Kazadi had been slain were false.

"Kazadi came, threw his arms around me, and we wept," Graber recalled later. "He was still recovering from the shock of all he had lost. He said, 'Do you remember all those acres of coffee plantation? I put all that I had into it to keep it nice for five years, expecting a crop this year; and all of it is lost. I don't care if my eyes never behold a coffee tree again; it would bring back to me all those sad memories. But God be praised, we still have our lives. The Great One will show us a way to start over again.' "

CPRA workers helped Kazadi build a house; they poured a concrete floor slab, erected a wooden wall-and-roof framework, and covered it all with sheets of corrugated metal roofing. Kazadi found four other AIMM pastors who had arrived as refugees; Archie gave them powdered milk to distribute to the most hungry.

"Every evening we pastors met to pray," Kazadi explained. "We cried to God loudly, with tears; suffering had brought us to the end of ourselves. Slowly, other Christians from here and there joined us. My mind told me to gather together these tormented sheep, and to establish a place for them to worship and pray. One day my fellow-pastors said, 'You are the eldest among us. You were leading us at the place from where we came. Accept to be our leader again. We'll help each other. We'll work together for our God.' So we hunted for a place to worship.''

They found a ramshackle shed — rusting, restraightened, nail-punctured sheets of corrugated roofing fastened onto crooked posts, all leaning leeward. The owner planned to remodel it into a bar but did not mind its being used meanwhile for a house of worship. It was pulled straight with a CPRA truck and reinforced for safety. There Kazadi established a church.

Graber agonized over the problem of food. The Kalonji government showed little concern for the appalling needs of its people. The commissioner of refugees had issued strict orders that churches stay out of the food-distributing business; Archie continued to distribute from his limited stocks virtually in secret. On July 10 he visited Mwena Ditu and found in the U.N. warehouse ample quantities of corn flour, rice, beans, and dried fish. The Kalonji government said only six of its trucks remained in running condition, and little of their time could be devoted to food distribution. Archie and a visiting agriculture expert visited government authorities to impress upon them the need for decisive action to curb famine. Archie gained a personal interview with President Kalonji himself and urged him to expedite the transportation of food.

''I'm grieved that people are suffering from hunger,'' the president said. ''But we cannot procure spare parts for trucks that are broken down; and for much of the time, trucks that are still running must be used for military purposes.''

Kalonji was occupied with what seemed to him more urgent matters. He was pressed to desperate ends to stay in power. On July 13 he accused Prime Minister Ngalula and several government officials of Ngalula's clan of sabotaging his authority. He removed them all from office and sent them to prison.

George Kiner, a CPRA executive inspecting the agency's work in South Kasai, visited Mwena Ditu on August 7. ''At the old U.N. headquarters, a Kalonji government truck was loading food,'' he reported. ''I saw at least one thousand refugees milling about, hoping to pick up grains that had broken through bags. The government had lines of soldiers around the area beating off the people with wooden clubs. Once in a while a soldier would throw a stick of dried fish toward them, as to the dogs, and then all the soldiers would laugh at the scrambling. It was sickening to watch."

On the following day King Kalonji returned from a conference in Leopoldville. An enormous crowd met him at the airport. He put on a red crown, climbed into a sedan chair, and was carried through the streets in glory. People honored him by dancing and singing in the streets all night. To the impartial observer, the inescapable question was how long the charade could survive.

Meanwhile CPRA responsibilities in Bakwanga were changing hands. Rocke had left in June for a short furlough in view of reassignment. He was replaced by two area Presbyterian missionaries, Day Carper and George Stewart, who helped on a part-time basis. Graber prepared to leave for the States in mid-August for a four-month furlough. Carrol Stegall, a seveny-year-old retired Presbyterian missionary, returned to Congo to take charge during Graber's absence.

As Archie transferred his work to Stegall, he took a mental inventory of all that had happened since his arrival the previous October. These had been the most tumultuous, emotion-packed ten months of his life. Some things he had never gotten used to: boorish menacing soldiers at roadblocks . . . the mercurial opportunistic politicians . . . a social order perpetually threatened by endemic thievery and violence. He could never forget the suffering of the people: a parentless family of five children, the oldest about nine, all suffering various stages of kwashiorkor . . . twenty-seven babies in a hospital with pneumonia and no clothing or blankets . . . some families still sleeping outside where it was damp and cold.

Bad news added a footnote to Archie's final days. On July 30 he received word that Charlesville station had been pillaged; to him it was almost as if his child had died. On August 15 he learned that the Baluba town at Lake Munkamba had been burned to the ground again, including the thirty-seven tents CPRA had left there.

But the good things that had happened far offset the bad. He would never forget the picture of those U.N. planes circling over Bakwanga, like ravens bringing food to Elijah. There weren't so many hollow-eyed, bloated-bellied children any more; now many of them were laughing and playing around little shelters they called home.

Never before had Archie seen such hunger for the Scriptures. He had opened a bookstore at Mwena Ditu and furnished resident village evangelists with wooden cases of Bibles for sale. Business was brisk. A pastor was in the road with the bookmobile every day selling Christian literature and conducting evangelistic services. Who should Archie find in church one day but old Chief Ilolo, one of those who had conspired to get his head when he was at Charlesville twenty-five years earlier. The old man wanted a Bible!

Graber's building supply program was now providing employment for about fifty heads of families; it was spawning small businesses; men would buy the tools they used, take them home, and set up their private after-hours workshops. The program stirred to life a spirit of enterprise and vigor which seemed contagious.

Archie never ceased to marvel at the capacity of the Baluba people to absorb suffering and then to rise up again. They were somehow driven by the feeling that if they could just make it over this or that difficulty, it would be better further on. He remembered a church service where a choir of refugees who had lost everything rose to sing their special number. It was a song Evelyn had translated years before: "Sail on. . . . Sail on."

"I have so much to be thankful for," he wrote before leaving on furlough. "Why was I born in a good Christian home, and not in a mud hut to parents who were pagan? Why do I know Jesus in my heart when so many know only fear and darkness and sin? Why do I rest every night in a warm, comfortable bed when so many are homeless and sleep on the ground outside? Why has God marvelously protected me so that I am not numbered with the many I've seen dead along the roadside? How can I, with all these blessings, criticize these people? How can I rest at ease and say that my job here is done? The Baluba say, 'If your child burns down your house, do you throw him into the fire?' They need encouragement, not criticism. Truly the fields here are white unto harvest. There are opportunities to serve here like we will never see again."

22

... Prison Camp ...

IF BALUBA REFUGEES in South Kasai were starting to emerge from their night of darkness when Archie left for the States in mid-August of 1961, Baluba refugees in Katanga Province were on the point of entering theirs.

The province of Katanga is larger than the states of Michigan, Indiana, Ohio, and Kentucky combined. It lies on the southeastern corner of what was then known as Congo. Its northwestern frontier bordered South Kasai. Its capital, Elisabethville, had a population of 110,000 in 1960; the city is located near the province's southeastern frontier, 1,200 miles across the country from the nation's capital of Leopoldville in Congo's western extremity.

The province has fabulous mineral wealth, in copper, cobalt, and uranium. Most of its natural resources are found in its southern quarter. Mining operations produced prosperous urban centers. The largest block of immigrants attracted to these industrial centers were Baluba from South Kasai, many of whom had achieved positions of leadership in their adopted society. By the end of the colonial era the population was relatively urbanized; over one-third of its people had moved from their traditional villages to larger centers and were wage earners.

When political independence loomed on the horizon, a coalition of principal tribes in the industrial area of Katanga formed the political party known as CONAKAT. It claimed to be the only party authorized to represent the province of Katanga, and threatened to suppress by force subversive efforts by non-Katangese. Its claim to political authority provoked tribes of North Katanga (principally of Baluba origin, but having little in common with the Baluba of South Kasai) to form an opposition party known as BALUBAKAT. CONAKAT's threat to suppress any signs of disloyalty among non-Katangese strained relationships with Baluba from South Kasai.

When a CONAKAT government took control of the province in June 1960, the break with the north was complete. BALUBAKAT leaders aligned with Lumumba. Politically inspired youth gangs in North Katanga terrorized the countryside with village burnings, tortures, and massacres. Katangan government troops pursued them.

When CONAKAT leader Tshombe announced his break from Congo on July 11, 1960, and assumed his powers as president of Katanga, annual mine taxes of $40 million were diverted from the Central Government into his own government treasury. His law forces consolidated his position by suppressing any signs of opposition. Their close scrutiny of Baluba and other non-Katangans heightened tensions and provoked isolated incidents of violence. Kalonji's break with Tshombe and alignment with the Central Government in April 1961 further spawned ill will between the Tshombe government and Baluba residing in Katanga.

Thus the stage was set for the tragic drama which began in August 1961. For each of the antagonists — the BALUBAKAT, the Tshombe government, the Belgians, and the United Nations — stakes were high.

In mid-August the United Nations Assembly in New York ordered the removal of 8000 Belgian military personnel from Katanga, who, it felt, were keeping Tshombe in power. The 250-man Swedish battalion in Elisabethville began to implement the U.N. resolution. Tensions mounted. Katangan soldiers, in efforts to tighten security, began to abuse and arrest Baluba residents. On Saturday, August 26, about 20 Baluba families came to the Swedish military camp on the outskirts of the city saying their lives were in danger for political reasons. U.N. troops gave them refuge. On Sunday, 200 families arrived with the same plea. On Monday, 750 families appeared. Since the Swedes could not contain this number within the barbed-wire-fence perimeter of the camp, they allowed refugees to settle outside it.

At this same time, prisoners at the provincial penitentiary, just over a mile from the camp, rioted, overpowered their guards, and

Moise Tshombe (front center), former president of Katanga Province, now called Shaba Province

Albert Kalonji, self-proclaimed Baluba king, former president of South Kasai Province.

A typical hut at the Elisabethville refugee camp *(MCC)*

Refugees lined up for food at the Elisabethville camp *(MCC)*

Women crowding fences to receive U.N. emergency food allotments (MCC)

opened the prison doors. Over 350 escaped. Among them were political prisoners, common-law prisoners, enemy soldiers accused of atrocities, and BALUBAKAT gang members accused of terrorist activities in North Katanga. These escapees fled to the U.N. Swedish headquarters, pleaded asylum as political prisoners, and were accepted.

Hostilities between Katangan and U.N. troops broke into open warfare in early September. By the time a cease-fire was announced on September 20, the population of the refugee camp encircling the headquarters of U.N. Swedish troops had swelled to over 30,000. Its two principal tribal groups were Baluba from South Kasi (40 percent) and tribespeople from North Katanga, the domain of BALUBAKAT (25 percent).

At first U.N. authorities anticipated that the dislocation would be temporary. Refugees with employment, fearing the uncertain hours of night, moved their most valuable possessions to the camp — automobiles, motorbikes, sewing machines, finer furniture; they slept there, and during the day returned to their jobs in town.

Many other refugees had nowhere to go. They scavenged the area for material to build shelters. They felled trees for limbs and branches; they ripped metal roofing off farm buildings and homes evacuated by Belgians. Within a few weeks, what had been a beautiful botanical landscape was transformed beyond recognition; only its tall conical ant hills remained. In its place were acres of ugly, congested squatter shelters of pasteboard, tin, burlap, and grass.

With the outbreak of war, all refugees were confined to the camp. There they fell under control of its inside forces. Now under U.N. protection, political extremists within the two main tribal groupings resumed subversive activities against the Katanga government and began fighting each other.

Terrorist youth gangs were reorganized and served political activists to control camp population. Among their chief weapons were hardwood clubs with large spikes driven laterally through one end, and sharpened bicycle chains which, when used as flails, quickly ground through human flesh and reduced legs to stems of bare bone. Internees who showed friendliness across tribal lines or who reported youth gang activities to U.N. authorities were branded "traitors" and were tortured or executed.

The Katanga government saw the refugee camp as a serious threat.

Not only was the camp a haven for political subversives, but forced absenteeism of highly skilled workers threatened the province's economy. When a government ultimatum for workers to return to their jobs went unheeded, the president approved a decree on October 19 ordering that all entrances to and exits from the camp be closed. This exacerbated feelings of bitterness toward the Katanga government, strengthened the positions of camp political groups seeking its overthrow, and compounded the misery of the refugees.

The camp became a living hell. Hemp-smoking youth gangs extended their acts of barbarism at will. Escaped criminals robbed and murdered. Katangan snipers hiding behind ant hills shot into the camp; during September their bullets claimed two hundred victims. In a tribal battle, which purportedly began over use of a water tap, fifty were killed. Still, even in this environment, the necessary physical processes of life continued. Over two hundred babies were born in the camp every month. Sanitary facilities were confined to a few private latrines. Hunger changed reasonable men into desperados; they slipped out of the camp at night, vandalized businesses, burglarized homes, and terrorized the population. Katangan soldiers launched reciprocal attacks against the camp. The climate became such that during every waking hour, defenseless refugees lived on the jagged edge of terror.

Frequently braving sniper fire, U.N. personnel worked valiantly against overwhelming odds. In mid-October, Swedish troops forced refugees camped on three sides of their military headquarters to relocate in the common area in front of it, so as to reduce the danger of its being overrun by armed refugees. The 250 U.N. soldiers were totally inadequate for camp security. To increase their control, they began using armored cars, which looked like tanks on rubber-tired wheels. They patrolled the camp perimeter. They made periodic forays into the camp to quell gang violence. Once, in fighting themselves free from tribal terrorists, they killed twenty-five.

U.N. personnel made barbed-wire-fenced corridors from the camp to points where they were distributing food; they used armed soldiers and police dogs to discourage rioting by those crazed with hunger. Political agitators frustrated efforts of the U.N. by issuing countermanding orders. They spread the rumor that food was poisoned, and refugees refused to come for it. Health officials calculated the camp was somehow absorbing 15 tons of fecal matter and 7,500 gallons of urine daily;

they feared the imminent outbreak of an epidemic. A barracks was converted into a hospital; here, under extreme handicaps, Italian U.N. personnel cared for the ill and victims of camp violence who dared come for help. To one side was a fenced-off area where refugees could mourn over their dead. Occasionally strong men would have to subdue someone going insane with grief. Burial sites were marked by a few personal effects of the deceased, such as an enamel plate or a shoe. At the end of four months, a cemetery area on one side of the camp was dappled with nine hundred graves.

Following the September war, negotiations between the United Nations and the Katanga government to solve the refugee problem were stalled by insurmountable hurdles. During October and November representatives from the U.N., from the government, and from large companies tried every inducement to get refugees to return to their homes and jobs. All efforts failed. These representatives agreed that camp internees must be reintegrated into the population of Katanga. The refugees unanimously disagreed. ''We prefer to die standing, rather than to live on our knees,'' they said. They were determined never again to bow to Katangan authority.

During December, war between Katangan and U.N. forces broke out again. By Christmas of 1961, the camp had begun to resemble a ticking time bomb. Its population had swelled to an estimated 50,000. The atmosphere was so poisoned that no U.N. personnel entered the camp without a submachine gun or a heavy revolver. A U.N. Social Affairs officer said that a white man entering the camp unarmed was asking to be executed.

Ironically, U.N. forces, by their humanitarian efforts, had incubated a self-feeding monster that was now beyond their power to contain — a snarling behemoth whose internal agonies could at any moment send it raging to annihilate them and to destroy an entire city. Why did U.N. forces in such a vulnerable position remain? None of the tribal or political groups where authority was centered wanted them. They were powerless to alter the worsening situation. They stayed because they felt their presence was crucial to forestalling a blood bath; they would try to hold on until some solution to the camp problem was found.

Archie Graber and his family boarded a plane in New York City and left for Congo on December 26. Because it was not safe for Irma and Nancy to live with Archie at Bakwanga, they would remain in

Leopoldville. Irma was delighted to return to the field. While she could not live with Archie, she would be closer to him and would see him when he visited the city on business. Moreover, she would be involved in the work of the mission again; she was to be housemother to six AIMM children who needed to live in the city during the school year.

Graber settled his family in Leopoldville and flew up-country to Bakwanga. He learned that forces of reason in the Kalonji government had again prevailed; its authorities had asked CPRA staff to help them distribute food to hospitals and dispensaries. Catholic Bishop Nkongolo could hardly refuse relief food offered under the auspices of his government; Catholic institutions gratefully accepted the participation of CPRA.

In February Graber was called to the Leopoldville offices of the Methodist church.

"As you know, our church has a long-established mission work in the province of Katanga," the executive secretary explained. "An extremely difficult situation has developed with a camp of some 50,000 refugees on the edge of Elisabethville. I understand that the majority of these people are Baluba from South Kasai. Our mission has worked in the city for many years; President Tshombe is a member of the Methodist church there. Unfortunately, this aligns us with the Katanga government in such a way that Baluba from South Kasai will not accept our efforts to help. U.N. people who supervise the camp are looking for a person who understands the culture and language of the Baluba people to function as a mediator. They say such a person is crucial to their finding a way to resolve the camp problem. U.N. authorities here in Leopoldville are aware of the work you have been doing with Baluba refugees at Bakwanga. They are wondering if you would go to Elisabethville to offer your services to U.N. personnel there."

Archie's response was immediate: "If you think I might be able to help, and you make arrangements for my trip, I'll go."

Plans for the trip were finalized at a meeting with Leopoldville U.N. officials on February 28. Graber flew to Elisabethville on March 19. A U.N. representative met him and took him to the office of Chief Coordinator of Refugee Work, Nils Gussing. There he received a lengthy briefing.

"We hope your work will help us recover the confidence of the refugees that we want to help them," Gussing explained. "Learn all you can about their thinking. You might try to survey the number of those originating from South Kasai.''

Archie took lodging in the city, in the guesthouse of the Methodist mission. His first Sunday morning there he preached at the Methodist church. He spoke in the Baluba language through an interpreter. On the following morning, when he returned to his office in the military headquarters on the camp perimeter, a small group of Christian Baluba men appeared. They greeted him by name and shook hands.

''Preacher, some of us were in church where you spoke yesterday. Our hearts split with happiness when we heard a white man speak in our language. We want to have a meeting with you tomorrow. We'll come and get you. We've got a lot to tell you. We have had no one to listen to us the past seven months that we have been here. Then when we're all finished talking, we want you to preach for us. Can you bring us some Bibles or New Testaments we can keep to read?''

''I'll be waiting for you here,'' he agreed.

They came the next afternoon and led Graber into the camp. Daily rains were turning it into a stinking quagmire. Women, their faded, dirty dresses soaked, and ill-clad children, their skin wet with rain, squatted shivering in their pitiful shelters. He was led to a hovel where about fifteen men were waiting. Among them were friends he had not seen since his years at Charlesville. For a few brief moments, refugees forgot their wretched conditions and rejoiced. Then they sat down in a circle and began to talk.

''I heard them out,'' Archie wrote later. ''It was the worst story of misery and filth and sickness and fear and fighting and death I ever heard in my thirty-one years in Congo. I thought about the cry of the psalmist, 'No man cared for my soul' (Ps. 142:4).''

He ministered the Word of God to them, prayed with them, and left.

Refugees had organized prayer meetings a few nights a week. They begged Archie to join them. He began attending regularly. He was deeply moved by the sincerity of their prayers.

''Greatest of All Spirits,'' they would cry, ''don't You see how we are suffering here? We have no homes. We have no decent place to lay down our bodies at night. Hunger is tormenting us. Enemies want to kill us. People in this city all have bad hearts toward us. God of love, aren't You strong enough to take us out of here? If You ever deliver us from this place of torment and set our feet down in the land of our ancestors, we'll be Your slaves perpetually.''

Graber questioned their plea to emigrate.

"What would you do if you went to South Kasai?'' he asked them. "No jobs are there for you. That land also is suffering from hunger and war.''

The Baluba responded with a fable:

"In the beginning of the world, all the animals, little and big, were living together happily. Then one day the lion came. He devoured some animals and wounded others. All the rest of the animals fled to the corners of the world to escape him. After a while the lion felt sad and lonely. He wanted to make friends again. So he pulled out his claws and practiced talking with a gentle voice. Then he went to the animals. He flattered them and promised he would be kind. But all the other animals remembered his cruelty; they remembered that he had killed their relatives. They renounced his friendship forever.

"No matter how the Katanga government hides its claws, or what it promises,'' they affirmed, "we will never trust it again.''

On days when there were prayer meetings, Graber would go into the camp after work in the late afternoon and leave at night. He noticed no threats to his safety. News of his visits spread to terrorist elements within the camp. They suspected that his activities might threaten their control of the refugees.

"Why are you allowing that white man to pass back and forth among us?'' they asked Baluba Christians.

"He's our friend . . . a missionary we sat with years ago before we ever came here.''

"Don't you know who he is working for?'' they rejoined. "The U.N. is paying that man to deceive you. With a friendship like that, you're hunting yourselves trouble.''

"We don't understand this U.N. business,'' Christians replied, "but we know this man. He is a worker for God. Look at all the months we've sat here in our suffering. Who has listened to us? We've had not one bit of hope. Now our friend of long ago appears. You tell us to drive him out? He's a relative of ours. He has a heart to help us.''

Periodically through the course of those weeks Gussing would call Graber for consultation.

"I understand that you are in the refugee camp alone at night," Gussing said once.

"That's right."

"It is my understanding that you have been warned of the danger of going into the camp unarmed, and particularly after dark."

"Yes, the U.N. soldiers warned me. But a lot of people in there are my friends. They're watching after me."

"That is a risk you must accept responsibility for. What do refugees feel is the answer to their problem?"

"The feeling is unanimous that they must return to their home country."

"You understand that these refugees represent a substantial part of the work force in Elisabethville industry; many of them were in key positions. It has been our judgment that removing them would wreck the economy. We have felt that if the political crisis were resolved, these people would want to return to their homes and jobs."

"Mr. Gussing, I've explained to them many times that there is no work for them in South Kasai. They insist that everything here is already lost; wherever they are, they will have to start from zero again. They will not consider starting over again in a land where their future is so insecure. They simply will hear nothing but that they leave and return to their homelands."

"Have you estimated the number of refugees who would want to go to Kasai?"

"I've registered 4,500 families in the strictly Baluba section of the camp. That would figure to something like 30,000 refugees; but I'm sure there are many more than that."

"South Kasai has already absorbed an enormous number of refugees. How do you think the population there would receive another 30,000?"

"These are their kinfolks," the missionary explained. "If we could get these people back to their localities of origin, the population there would receive them with open arms and share with them what little they have."

On March 30 five top authorities of the U.N. Congo operation met in Elisabethville. With Graber they flew to Bakwanga to explore the possibility of relocating the camp refugees. The Kalonji government assured them its full cooperation. Then the team visited villages in the area to determine how such a number of refugees would be received. The people were more than generous.

"They are all our tribemates," they responded. "Many of us have blood relatives in that camp. Why would we not welcome them?"

During the entire month of April planners studied logistics for the operation. Transporting this number of people over eight hundred miles of deteriorating dirt roads by truck convoy was virtually out of the question. Transporting them by train to Mwena Ditu was impossible because of a dynamited bridge close to the South Kasai border. Either of these options was dangerous because North Katangans were pro-Lumumba, and enemies to Baluba from South Kasai. Transporting them all by air directly to Bakwanga was prohibitively expensive.

Graber's contact was with a mere handful of the refugee population. He informed his friends of efforts being made to relocate them to South Kasai. Rumor of the plan quickly spread through the camp. The idea was not popular with political gangsters whose terrorizing gripped the masses. During one of Archie's meetings the conflict came to a head.

"How do we know you aren't deceiving these people?" someone in the crowd called out. "We all know that you work for the U.N."

"Sufficient money to take all these thousands of people out of here and put them in South Kasai," grumbled another, "where would it come from? You say that the U.N. is going to show us that kind of love? Have we ever seen the U.N. do anything good for us before? Ridiculous!"

"We've got their ruse figured out," affirmed another. "The U.N. and the Katangans want to get rid of this camp. They don't care about us. After we entrust ourselves to them, they'll take us out somewhere and annihilate us."

They spoke their feelings and fell silent. The white man paused a few moments; then he answered.

"I am a worker for God. I arrived in this land before some of you who are talking were born. Ever since then I've been working to help black people. Show me one person who ever said I deceived him. Do you think that after all these years, I'm going to start deceiving people today? Before your eyes I affirm that I'm taking the burden of all of you upon my shoulders. If anyone is killed or wounded because we have deceived him, the blood of that person will be on my hands."

Response was spontaneous.

"Well said, preacher!"

"We're with you!"

"Keep going ahead!"

"We're praying for you, person of God!"

Efforts to organize the mass relocation culminated in a meeting on 5 May 1962 at the Swedish military headquarters on the edge of the camp. Robert Gardiner, officer-in-charge of U.N. Congo operations, ten other top-echelon U.N. officials, and Graber were present. During the course of the meeting, there was a flurry of phone calls and telegrams to faraway places. Washington, D.C., was contacted to clear use of U.S. Air Force Globemasters. Plans were finalized: refugees would be shipped by military-protected train half the distance north to an air base at Kamina; from there they would be flown by Globemaster to Bakwanga. If the possibility opened, others would be airlifted directly to Bakwanga.

The following day, Sunday, Archie preached to Baluba camp refugees. Then he announced that arrangements were completed; soon they would be leaving for South Kasai.

They were jubilant. They clapped. They leaped. They wept.

"The God of the Israelites has heard our wailing!"

"The Spirit-Creator of our forefathers has shown us mercy!"

Spontaneously they broke into song:

"Be not distressed whatever comes;

God will take care of you. . . ."

"God stay with you till we meet again. . . ."

They hadn't packed a thing. But in spirit they were already on their way.

23

... Let's Go Home ...

ON THE EVE of May 8, 1962, Archie ate supper, returned to his guesthouse sleeping room, and sat down in front of his typewriter. His body ached with fatigue, but his spirits soared.

"The first trainload of 1,028 refugees left the depot at 3:30 this afternoon," he wrote. "What a thrill it was to see them go! They were so happy to leave this place that they were literally shouting for joy. There are two flatcars loaded with sandbags in front of the steam engine to keep it from being derailed by a mine explosion. Directly behind the engine is a flatcar loaded with an armored car and soldiers manning machine guns. Then come the open-windowed passenger cars. There is another armed flatcar like the first one in the center of the train, and another one on the end. As I write this letter I can picture that long train winding its way around the Congo hills, taking these refugees to what they see as their 'promised land.' It will take twenty-four hours for them to reach Kamina, where they will be airlifted the rest of the way. We hope and pray that there will be no bloodshed, so that this can be the first train of many. A lot of people are wondering how long it will be until we can say, 'There goes the last of the refugee camp.'"

It was clear now that forces in the camp willing to cooperate with the U.N. were prevailing. Many refugees were eager to leave. Graber was sent to Bakwanga to make arrangements on the receiving end. He simply reopened his ministry of relocating refugees. He gathered a team of refugee pastors to help him. They scouted the countryside; they cataloged rural areas which could be occupied, and the number of refugees the local residents of each area were willing to receive. One

211

chief and his clan leaders decided they could handle ten thousand; another chief agreed to receive four thousand.

"Team members decided against reopening a refugee camp at Bakwanga. They pooled results of their survey and established seven key transit points in receiving areas. Upon arrival at the Bakwanga airport, refugees would be transported directly by truck to the transit point nearest their place of origin, where relatives or clansmen could come and receive them. CPRA gave an initial supply of food and a Scripture booklet to each family.

One day Archie caught a U.N. flight to Leopoldville to spend a weekend with his family. Irma looked forward to these visits. They were so rare. She had hoped her coming to Congo would mean that she would see him frequently, but it didn't turn out that way. She found it difficult to fill the role of substitute mother and father for seven missionary schoolchildren. She needed Archie's support and encouragement.

But often, even when he was in Leopoldville, she saw little of him. Take that Saturday for example. All day long he was busy in offices of the U.N. and the Congo government, taking care of business regarding evacuation of the Elisabethville refugees. So Irma planned something special for Sunday. All the offices would be closed, and Archie would be free. She would prepare dishes Archie especially liked, and their big family would have a wonderful noon meal together with Archie at the head of the table.

She got up promptly Sunday morning and worked hard after breakfast to prepare everything she could before leaving for church. They piled the children into the car and went to church together. She treasured those moments . . . the quietness of the worship service and sitting beside her husband. After the benediction, people exited leisurely and mingled in the front yard visiting. Irma and Archie were separated in the crowd; she chatted with some friends while she waited for him to return. She was anxious to gather the children and be on their way home for dinner.

"Irma."

Archie had approached her from behind.

"I'm sorry, but I won't be able to come to dinner."

"Why not?"

"There is an important U.N. official who wants to have the noon meal with me. He has business to talk over with me about the refugees."

"Can't he see you some other time?"

"That's what I asked him. He says this is the only time he can see me. I'll be home just as soon as I can get there."

Irma was crushed. She tried to act brave. She gathered her brood into the car and went home. It was all she could do to keep from breaking up. The children were delighted with the special meal, but her appetite had largely vanished. When Archie returned in the late afternoon, she was too deeply hurt to relate to him. He quickly sensed something was wrong. At a moment when they were alone, he broached the subject.

"Irma, what's the matter?"

"Oh, nothing." She bit her lip to keep back tears.

"There *is* something the matter." He frowned at her searchingly.

Archie took his place at the head of the table for supper. They ate leftovers. Irma was still uncommunicative. He helped her clear the dishes off the table and then said, "I think it's time for us to go for a ride. Let's drive up to the monument."

They left the older children to do the dishes, got into the car, and followed the winding road that leads to the highest point of elevation in the city. They got out of the car and climbed, hand in hand, up broad stairs to a concrete terrace on the rim of the hill. Centered on the far edge of the terrace was a huge pedestal. Upon it, life-size, stood the explorer Henry Stanley, silently peering under a bronze hand westward, across the vast quiet pool which bore his name, toward where the river narrows and begins tumbling on the final leg of its journey to the Atlantic. They walked to one side of the monument and leaned on the concrete balustrade, which enclosed the front edge of the terrace. They were alone. The evening was still. The view was magnificent. Darkness was enfolding the river pool. On its right shore, tops of modern buildings protruded above the trees. Their lights were beginning to blink on. The two of them took it all in for a while. Then Archie broke the silence.

"Irma, we're not going down off this hill until you tell me what's bothering you."

She looked down nervously at her arm and then out across the distant water again.

"Now what is it?"

She finally mustered courage to articulate her feelings. Her voice choked.

"You're so occupied with your work. . . . Nancy and I . . .

sometimes we wonder if we have a daddy and husband any more.''

The impact of her words moved him deeply. After a moment of silence he spoke.

''Dear, when I offered to help settle refugees, I had no idea what it would mean. I don't enjoy being out in the road living out of a suitcase all of the time any more than you do. But what can I do? There are all those thousands of suffering people who need my help. There are important men whom I must see if I'm going to help them. But God hasn't called just me to the refugee work. He has also called you to care for these missionary children. It is awfully hard for both of us. But for the time being, it just has to be this way. It won't be this way forever, and He's promised to give us grace to carry these burdens. Why don't we have prayer and recommit ourselves to the Lord? Let's ask Him to give us help for the work He's given us to do at this time.''

They bowed their heads. Archie prayed.

''Our Father, when we agreed to do this work, You knew what was ahead. You love us. You wouldn't call us to bear a burden that is too great for us. We both long for the day when we can live together as a family again. But for right now, help us to be willing to make this sacrifice so that people who are suffering so much more than we can be helped. You've called each of us to important tasks. We recommit ourselves to You right now. We trust You to make us strong so that we can do our tasks well. We pray in the Name of Jesus. Amen.''

He turned to look at her. There were tears. He took her into his arms and kissed her. He held her close until the warmth of their love had melted away all the feelings of tension. Then he released her. They walked back to the car and got in. Then they drove down the hill and back to their duties in the world again.

On Monday Graber was called into the office of Robert Gardiner, chief of U.N. operations in the Congo.

''When you were here Saturday,'' he said, ''you spoke of the need for heavy-duty transport trucks to carry refugees from the Bakwanga airport to the resettlement areas.''

''Yes.''

''I have lined up ten trucks here that are available for your use. Could you find drivers to take them inland?''

Archie found nine missionaries in the capital city looking for a way to go up-country. They were willing to drive the white U.N. trucks inland. Each of them was allowed to load a limited quantity of supplies and personal effects into his truck. The threat of war in one area made it impossible for them to make the full eight-hundred-mile trip by road. To by-pass the area, they loaded the trucks onto a river barge and made a seven-day voyage to Port Francqui, the river port where the Ghanian troops had been massacred. There were still 330 miles of dirt road between them and Bakwanga.

Two truckloads of U.N. soldiers and an armored car escorted the truck convoy for the 240-mile road trip to Luluabourg. It arrived without incident. On June 2, the morning after the convoy arrived at Luluabourg, missionary drivers reorganized their loads and prepared for the last leg of their journey — the 90-mile trip across Lulua–Baluba frontier country to Bakwanga. The military escort wanted to accompany them. Recalling feelings which prevailed between U.N. military personnel and soldiers of Kalonji, Graber refused the offer. This proved to be fortunate. They began the journey in mid-afternoon. That was a mistake.

Graber drove the lead truck. June is at the end of the rainy season. Roads were gullied and awash with sand. Progress was slow. Darkness found them still deep in Lulua country. As the trucks approached the trouble-plagued frontier at Lake Munkamba where there was customarily a roadblock, Archie grew increasingly tense.

"O God," he began praying, "keep us from the hands of wild soldiers tonight. See that these trucks get through to Bakwanga safely."

He crossed the tribal frontier. It was now midnight. In the pitch darkness he encountered no roadblock. Did any of the other trucks meet difficulty? It was almost too easy. Still, Archie felt somewhat relieved now, for they were in Baluba country. He proceeded for about nine miles, wended his way down a familiar hillside, and reached a river bridge. This would be a good place to make sure everybody was still accounted for. He stopped the truck. Other trucks pulled up and stopped behind him. He walked from truck to truck, checking with each driver and counting. There were still ten. He praised the Lord, returned to his truck, climbed into the cab, and rumbled his way across the bridge.

Less than a mile ahead his lights picked up a heavy pole supported by forked sticks. Archie approached the roadblock. As he was braking to a stop, suddenly six soldiers with rifles leaped from the roadside into the illumination of his headlights and yelled:

"Stop!"

They froze in their positions, tensed for combat.

Archie prayed. Cautiously, he opened the cab door and stepped onto the road. They held him at gunpoint.

"Life to you," he spoke in the Baluba language. "What are you looking for?"

"Where are the soldiers?" one of the armed men shouted.

"What soldiers?"

"You are driving U.N. trucks. Where are the soldiers?"

"We are not hauling soldiers."

"You're lying!" another snarled, quietly stepping in closer to fix his rifle toward Graber's stomach. "We saw you stop at the bridge. You didn't stop there for nothing. You left your truckloads of soldiers off there so that we wouldn't catch you. At this time they're already cutting through the high grass on foot on their way toward Bakwanga."

"Friends, I am a speaker of God. My work is not to haul soldiers who fight with people. I came to South Kasai to help the refugees in their suffering. In all my passing back and forth through this country, haven't you heard about me?"

"If you aren't hauling soldiers, what are you hauling?"

"Just a few of our things."

"So you are a 'speaker of God' bringing into our country in the name of the U.N. many trucks with their insides empty," the sergeant in command remarked sardonically. "Then why are you trying to pass through here in the middle of the night? This is the time when people with good hearts are in their houses sleeping."

"I have a good heart," Archie replied. "We have to get these trucks to Bakwanga soon. Refugees are arriving there . . . your tribemates, who were suffering terribly in a prison camp in Elisabethville. We want to transport them to their villages so they can get settled. Let me show you my path papers. I am a friend of Chief Kalonji. To prove that my words are true, some of you can get into my truck and ride with us to Bakwanga; in the morning we'll go see Chief Kalonji."

They took his papers, looked at them, and began debating among themselves what to do.

"Where did he get such papers?"

"They could be fraudulent. You know the clever tricks of the U.N."

"But he says he's a missionary, a friend of President Kalonji."

"That's a story he's made up to escape."

"Did you ever see a missionary driving trucks of the U.N.? Missionaries drive trucks of the mission."

"But he talks our language like he has been here a long time."

"Then he's a collaborator with the U.N. The guilt is the same."

"The U.N. has bad blood toward us. Before we chased them out of here, we were killing each other."

"That's right. That many trucks full of soldiers . . . it could be an invasion."

The sergeant commanded Archie: "Bring all the drivers. Stand them here in a line in front of your truck where we can see them."

Graber feared this was a first step toward their execution.

"Wait a bit!" he interjected. "Let's all go to your commanding officer. Where is he? Don't you want to go with us to Bakwanga? There you will be able to establish the truth of this matter."

"Shouldn't the commandant know what's happening here?" one of them suggested.

The sergeant pondered for a moment and agreed. He and another soldier would escort the white man alone to the commandant. Graber went back to leave word with each of the drivers in turn.

"We're in trouble. They're taking me to headquarters. Stay inside your truck . . . and *pray*."

An escort soldier climbed into the back of the truck. Graber climbed into the driver's seat, and the sergeant, holding his rifle, climbed into the cab beside him. The four other troops stayed to hold the nine trucks and drivers under cover of their guns. Graber's guard ordered him to turn left and drive the truck down a side path. The missionary's mind began spinning for a way to extricate himself. He didn't know where they were going. He drove slowly, fearing they would arrive too soon.

"Look, my friend," he began, "tell me what it is you want."

The soldier deliberated a moment.

"Do you have some money?"

"You know well that we missionaries have very little money." Archie reached into a hip pocket, took out his billfold, and handed it to him. "Take whatever you want from it; just let me go back to the other drivers. We're so tired; we want to be on our way."

The sergeant looked inside the billfold, found just over a dollar, took it, and returned the billfold. They drove on in silence.

Another thought occurred to Graber.

"There's a case of orange pop in the back of the truck. Why don't you take what you want?"

The soldier showed no interest.

The truck moved relentlessly onward.

"Look," Archie said again. "If you'll just let me go back and let us all go on our way, I'll see that you get a nice new watch."

The soldier, holding his rifle erect in front of him, stared stonily ahead into the darkness.

Graber groped for another approach. The soldier broke the silence.

"Stop at that fire ahead."

Archie's eyes caught a cluster of embers glowing in the darkness. He approached it and stopped. In the light of the embers he saw what appeared to be the form of a man stretched out in a sleeping position on a chair.

The sergeant got out of the cab, strode to the chair, coughed uncomfortably, snapped to attention, and saluted. Graber stood to one side of him. The officer grunted, arousing himself from sleep.

"Pshhhht." Archie recognized the sound. The second soldier, coming from the rear of the truck, had just pulled the cap off a bottle of pop with his teeth. He strode to the officer, snapped to attention, saluted, gave him the pop, and proceeded to stir the fire. The sergeant finished announcing their business just as the stirred embers broke into flame, throwing light onto the scene. The officer's eyes slowly followed up the white man's form to his face.

"Ki-i-i-ya! Preacher Lutonga! What are you doing here this time of night?"

He sat erect and reached to shake Graber's hand. This officer regularly patrolled the Bakwanga-Munkamba road — he knew Archie well. His soldiers manning the roadblock were new to the area. The officer exploited the occasion for leisurely conversation. Was Archie well? Where had he been? How were things in Leopoldville? How was work with the refugees progressing? Archie recognized the price of his release: to hold in strict check any sign of impatience and to reciprocate congenial chitchat until the man was satisfied.

The conversation was winding down when the commandant finally said, "It would be best if you would return to the roadblock and have the others drive their trucks here. That way I can examine the trucks and the path papers of each of the drivers."

The words intensified Archie's aching fatigue. He smiled and said, "Thank you, sir."

Graber, with the two soldiers, drove the four miles back to the roadblock and ordered the nine drivers to follow them to the command post. When the commandant had examined the papers of each man, he was satisfied. The escort soldiers climbed into Graber's truck, and they all drove back to the roadblock. The sergeant got out, ordered his men to open the roadblock, and came to Archie's side of the cab.

"I want you to know that if you had arrived here with any U.N. soldiers, not a person of you would have passed through here alive. Go on your way."

Graber nodded respectfully, started the truck, and riveted his eyes on the road ahead. They completed the journey with no further incident, and arrived at Bakwanga at 4:30 A.M. The trucks were put to use immediately to haul the steady flow of prison camp refugees from the Bakwanga airport to their respective places of origin.

Later in Elisabethville, it was not the threat of war that jeopardized Graber's life, but the real thing. He was inside the Methodist mission guesthouse in the city one evening when Katangan and U.N. troops tangled in one of their perennial battles. Mortars began booming. Shells whistled. Bullets zinged. It sounded as if he were caught in the crossfire. Archie had learned that just a few days earlier a Belgian had been cut to pieces a few doors from the guesthouse. Battle noises intensified to an ear-rending din. Archie was scared. In a desperate search for some protection, he crawled under the bed. He began praying.

"Father, I didn't expect to get caught in the middle of anything like this. Please get me out of here. You know how hard it is for Irma where she is. How could she ever carry on alone? I promised her the day would come when we could live together like a family again. I want to go back and be with her and Nancy and finish my promise."

About 9:30 P.M. there was a break in the battle. Graber heard the noise of approaching footsteps. He remembered the massacred Belgian. Someone knocked. Then the door opened — he'd forgotten to bolt it. Graber's first thought was to take flight; then he realized that there was no other exit.

"I guess it's my turn next," he told himself. "In just a short time I'll be with the Lord. I'll just lie quietly and let them find me here."

"Graber! Graber! Where are you?"

It was the voice of his missionary host.

"You're in the line of fire here. Grab your suitcase and follow me."

Archie scrambled out from under the bed, seized his suitcase, and raced behind his host through the darkness toward the lights of the missionary residence, stumbled and sprawled at its doorstep, picked himself up, and rushed inside.

On the following evening he was seated on the living room floor of the residence recording noises of the war, when a bullet struck the fireplace behind him. He picked it up and put it into his pocket for a souvenir. It was thirty-six hours before he could leave the house and resume the business of his trip.

Cargo planes, refugee trains, and transport trucks working together relocated a steady, heavy stream of refugees. A problem developed on June 24, when 1,500 refugees from a small tribe which borders the Baluba to the north arrived by train at Kamina, but refused to board planes for Bakwanga; they feared this last step was a trap set by the Baluba to catch and massacre them. Archie was asked to board the next flight from Bakwanga to Kamina. The fearful refugees were assembled in a stadium. Archie spoke to them over a truck-mounted public address system. By taking full responsibility for their safety upon himself, he convinced them to continue on their way. Within a few days they began arriving at Bakwanga.

Personnel supervising the operation at Elisabethville also encountered difficulties. The prison camp would not die easily. To its emotion-laden atmosphere was now added the turmoil of moving people. Every day refugees were killed and wounded in continuing violent clashes between camp factions. U.N. soldiers destroyed shacks of evacuating refugees and patrolled the camp perimeter to discourage any further influx of refugees. In spite of these things, harrassed tribesmen from the city kept slipping into the camp, increasing its population by thousands.

Graber shuttled between Bakwanga and Elisabethville to help keep the operation running smoothly. He assisted refugees preparing to leave.

"It is very hard to watch families sort through their few things and decide what they will have to leave in order to keep their weight down to what is allowed on the plane," he wrote. "Many had to leave hand tools they will need to make gardens. But there is nothing else for them to do. The U.N. is determined to get rid of this camp at any cost."

With this kind of determination, the program of refugee relocation moved steadily ahead. By June 8, one month after the first trainload left Elisabethville, refugees emigrating to South Kasai totalled 17,000. By the end of the month the number had climbed to 32,000.

On July 12, 1962, Archie and his family returned to Elisabethville from a brief South African vacation. They climbed onto one of the Globemasters airlifting refugees directly to Bakwanga. Old people, almost too feeble to climb up the ramp into the plane, carried their tiny, precious bundles. Families used various means to beat the weight-limit rule. Women wore several dresses. The abdomens of men protruded curiously with soft items they were carrying under their clothing. Children struggled to walk in their daddies' knee-boots, or wore coats with sleeves hanging to their knees. There was no panic. They accepted all that happened on the voyage with quiet, dignified resignation, even including the birth of babies.

At long last, local people enduring this terrible camp nightmare could say, "There goes the last of the refugees." Heaving a great, corporate sigh of relief, they watched it happen in late July. By the end of that month, 54,000 refugees had been relocated in Kasai; another 20,000 had been resettled in North Katanga; and the camp site was razed. The resettlement project cost the United Nations just over two million dollars.

The refugees were immensely grateful. Archie said that in spite of all they had lost, seldom did he hear anyone complain. Though their promised land proved a haven from many things, tension from competing political factions was not one of them. Only a few months after their repatriation, Kalonji's government fell, the autonomous Baluba kingdom was reintegrated as a province into the Congo, and former Prime Minister Ngalula, arch-rival to Kalonji for chieftainship of the Baluba, was elevated to the top post as governor of the province. These events forced the Baluba people to face their next crisis: Would supporters of deposed Kalonji abandon their dreams of ruling a Baluba kingdom and submit themselves to the authority of Governor Ngalula?

24

... Pain of Estrangement ...

NGALULA TOOK POWER as governor of the province on October 30, 1962. Village youth brigades fanatically loyal to Kalonji fled to the forest to hide. Within two months they were engaged in full-scale guerrilla warfare against Congolese occupation troops and the government of Ngalula.

The war flared, sputtered, and then flared again for months. It engulfed the western half of the province, where village population was of the Kalonji clan. By March 1963, 300,000 refugees were again homeless; for many of them, this was the third time within the span of eighteen months that they had lost their homes and taken refuge in the forest or high grass. Archie was made to wonder if the capacity of these people to suffer knew no limit.

Their ability to survive misfortune can be credited not so much to relief aid provided them as to their sheer, stubborn determination to triumph. Self-motivation, which Archie had seen emerge in the mid-1930s, had now blossomed into driving ambition. There was a bookseller who, when war reached his village, buried a large, metal footlocker of Christian literature in the dirt floor of his hut and fled. When the war passed, he returned, disinterred his inventory, and set up business again. A one-legged cripple would hobble past the CPRA residence every day and later return with a few sticks tied onto his crutches; he was building his house. A camp of hungry lepers to whom CPRA furnished food and cement made five thousand cement blocks to construct a new medical dispensary.

Christians transferred this same kind of resourcefulness and ambition to their work of building the church. They were starting a new thing. The Baluba forefathers used to say, "Even if pioneers begin only by swatting grasshoppers, one day their progeny will laud them for their marvelous feats." Kazadi sent fellow refugee pastors to survey the area and compiled a complete list of names and locations of Christians who had emigrated from the AIMM field. Believers planted in new villages established by Graber's refugee relocation program began gathering people for regular worship. Soon new churches were cropping up like fresh, green shoots from a burnt-off grassland. Kazadi subdivided the area and assigned each refugee pastor a parish of village churches. In May 1963 Kazadi gave Graber $1,200 of accumulated offering money, and CPRA workmen built the pastor a worship place of his own.

From their years in the AIMM field, Baluba leaders had learned how to do the work of the church. However, when they sought to reestablish themselves in South Kasai, they met with three problems for which they were little prepared. First, for over sixty years South Kasai had been the exclusive domain of the American Presbyterian Congo Mission; Protestant societies traditionally respected each other's borders. What was the status of this new body of immigrant believers? Second, what would be the continuing relationship between this fragment of the AIMM church now removed from its original geographic setting and the home board in America whose resources had given it birth and nurtured it? And finally, how would this fledgling Baluba church stand up under the stresses of infighting between the Ngalula and Kalonji clans?

Pastor Kazadi had no ambivalence about how to handle the first problem.

"I went to a conference of Presbyterian church leaders and told them that we Mennonites would be starting a work of our own," he reported. "At first they disputed the idea. I told them, 'From my childhood all the way to my present old age, I've been taught by the Mennonites. I've matured and ripened in their beliefs and traditions. If I go into a new church now, I'll return to my infancy to learn all over again its different way of doing things. Accept for us to be among you and do our work by ourselves.' We debated and discussed the matter in other meetings, until in June of 1963 we reached agreement that the Mennonites could begin a work by themselves."

The second problem could not be dispatched so easily. While the refugee Christians did not intend to unite with the Presbyterians, they made clear their intention to continue relations with AIMM. Graber had been blind to church labels; he had related ministries of CPRA to need wherever he found it. Regardless of the material benefits enjoyed from CPRA, refugees insisted that they were "AIMM Christians."

Refugee church leaders felt it incumbent upon the AIMM home board to share with them benefits which the church in the field from which they had been driven continued to enjoy. "Why can't you help *us* with our Bible school, or with medicine, or literature, or missionary personnel?" they kept asking. "Why should those who chased us out and lost so little continue to receive help, and we who lost everything receive none?"

In his correspondence, Archie repeatedly urged the home board not to abandon the refugee Christians in South Kasai. Personnel in the home office hesitated to risk stirring up ill will by supporting a separate work in the Presbyterian field. Moreover, AIMM national church administrative personnel headquartered at Tshikapa insisted that any unilateral aid from the home board to South Kasai would encourage a church split. Officials at the home end struggled with the problem. How could they respond to the needs of the AIMM refugee Christians in South Kasai without widening the breach between those refugee Christians and believers remaining in the original AIMM field? They failed to find a way out of the dilemma. Unsuspectingly, their inaction was encouraging the very thing they sought to avoid.

Because public education had always been the responsibility of missions working in Congo, mission schools were subsidized by government funds. Kazadi now set up a network of village schools to provide elementary education for children of AIMM refugees. He felt it essential to establish a reliable channel for the receipt of government subsidy funds so as to secure the future of the South Kasai Mennonite school system. An initial agreement to receive funds via the Presbyterian church did not prove satisfactory. His geographic separation from AIMM administrative offices at Tshikapa and feelings of tribal alienation which persisted ruled out those offices as a reliable channel. Kazadi was of the Ngalula clan. When South Kasai returned under the jurisdiction of the Central Government and Ngalula was made governor of the province, Kazadi recognized the moment as propitious.

"Kazadi called all Mennonite leaders to Bakwanga," reported a pastor who then lived twenty miles west of the city in the heart of Kalonji country. "He said that we should establish our own church and carry on. It appeared that our mother who had given us birth had forgotten us; so we agreed. He got papers from the Ngalula government, went to Leopoldville, and opened the path for us to begin receiving subsidy money for our schools. Things started going well. Then the war between Kalonji's youth and the army of the Central Government broke out. It sowed seeds of distrust and disrespect which split us in two. We church leaders from the Kalonji clan wanted one of our people to be among those who would represent our South Kasai Mennonite Church before government authorities. Kazadi refused. It appeared to us that he wanted the Mennonite church to be represented only by leaders from the Ngalula clan. Thus we no longer had a voice in things."

And so, the third problem of tribal infighting proved the most difficult of all.

Unfortunately, the kind of determined spirit Baluba found essential to their survival did not always make for the harmonious resolution of differing opinions. After the two groups failed to find a compromise, the rift grew. When guerrilla warfare of the pro-Kalonji youth was finally suppressed in mid-1964, Governor Ngalula was replaced by a man named Mukamba, who happened to be son-in-law to Kazadi. Shortly thereafter payment of subsidy funds to schools of the Kalonji clan was suspended. The AIMM administrative office at Tshikapa heeded the call of Kalonji-group Christians to come and mediate the problem. The Tshikapa office sent a delegation of leaders. The delegation arrived at the Bakwanga airport, were placed under house arrest by military police, and were sent back out on the next day's plane. The delegation and Kalonji-clan Christians suspected Kazadi's group of engineering these reverses in complicity with the governor. The groups of leaders next flew to Leopoldville, the nation's capital, to appeal to federal government officials to intervene in the matter of suspended payment of subsidy funds. They were unsuccessful.

"Then our delegation went a second time," the Kalonji-clan pastor continued. "Our spokesman got into the office of the minister of the interior and told him that if the problem was not resolved so that our children could go to school, there would be war between the two clans

again. This minister and the minister of education called leaders of the
Kazadi group and made leaders from both sides sign papers that subsidy
moneys would be divided between the two groups. Thus we of the
Kalonji clan continued working in harmony with our mother-church at
Tshikapa, and Kazadi kept working on his own.''

When a close relative of Kazadi who had influence with the Central
Government in Leopoldville secured legal recognition for the Kazadi
group, the break was complete. Each of the groups continued to press
aggressively forward in building the church of Jesus Christ, but they no
longer communicated with each other.

In July 1963, a different kind of separation was ended. After two
and one-half years of disrupted home life, Irma and Nancy joined Archie
at Bakwanga, and they began living together as a family again. In
outlying regions the guerrilla war sputtered on; but now the church-split
stemming from it caused Archie and Irma the greater pain. Since the
approach of political independence, brokenness of relations had caused
ghastly suffering and loss. Archie's exhaustive efforts had been for the
purpose of healing that brokenness. Now it reached to divide and
alienate those very people who were once its common victims. He was
reluctant to fix blame. He recalled the repeated waves of misfortune they
had survived. Was he sure that if he were one of them, he would act
differently? He watched with compassion, relating to both sides equally.
He tried to help them begin reaching toward each other again, but with
little apparent success.

CPRA officials in Leopoldville, watching the progressive rehabilitation of the Baluba of South Kasai, decided that the agency could
close its relief operations in Bakwanga by mid-1965. Since Graber's arrival in October 1960, he and his staff, furnished by Presbyterian and
Mennonite agencies, had compiled an impressive list of accomplish-
ments.[1]

Refugees had been reestablished and were self-supporting. The
CPRA team had constructed fifty-two school buildings, plus churches
and medical units. It had distributed some twenty-thousand baby chicks.

[1]In addition to personnel already mentioned: Glen Murray left his family in Dallas,
Texas, and for eighteen months was in charge of relief food distribution. Henry Braun,
Ron Peters, and Warren Yoder, young men doing relief work in lieu of military service,
were in charge of building construction and vehicle maintenance. For a two-year period,
Art Banman from Newton, Kansas, was responsible for the chicken project; and his
wife, Frieda, was cook and housekeeper for the team.

Twenty-four of Graber's workmen had built their own homes of permanent materials. Sixteen of his carpenters had bought their tools and started private businesses. By means of a profit-sharing plan, the black foreman who had been responsible for the CPRA carpenter shop, its power equipment and supplies, completed payment of a $45,000 purchase price and went into business on his own. All of these ministries had in a measure contributed to the remarkable growth of the church. In overall retrospect, Archie was gratified. Only the estrangement of the two groups of Baluba brethren remained to mar the picture. It was one thing, he saw, to build houses and classrooms and churches. To mend broken relationships was something else.

In early 1965, when Graber was in the process of closing down CPRA operations, he had occasion to return to the AIMM field and visit his old station at Charlesville.

"The ferry we had used to cross the river so many times wasn't there any more," he wrote poignantly. "It had been destroyed in tribal fighting. I crossed in a dugout canoe. I walked by the old brickyard on the river's edge where in past years hundreds of thousands of bricks were made; now it is all covered over with vines and jungle brush. Somehow, 'it just don't seem like home anymore.'

"I walked onto the station where well-kept roads, paths, and gardens lined with flowers once brought cheer to all who lived there; but grass and weeds have choked out the flowers and have left the roads like cow paths. Then I walked up to the village where once there was street upon street of African homes of mud walls and thatch roofs — homes where we had spent many pleasant evenings around bonfires. Now it looked like a deserted graveyard. I walked from mound to mound, recalling to mind the people who had once lived there. Now it is all silent and overgrown with weeds. 'It just don't seem like home any more.' "

The Graber's left Bakwanga in late May 1965 and went to the States. After an eight-month furlough they returned to Congo for another four years; Archie was assigned to refugee settlement and construction projects in other parts of the country. During these years he had only rare contact with people in Kasai. But they had not forgotten him. As the day approached for Archie and his family to leave Africa for what was understood to be their last time, AIMM church leaders at Tshikapa laid plans for a special day of farewell festivities on their behalf. It would be in May 1969, at Kalonda, the station Lutonga had built in the 1950s on the hillside just across the river from Tshikapa.

"As top leaders of the AIMM were planning for the farewell, I suggested that they might want to send an invitation to Kazadi," recalls James Bertsche, a veteran missionary then living at Kalonda. "There was notable lack of enthusiasm for it. They thought that feelings were still running too high; it wasn't yet the right time. We pressed the issue a bit further. Finally they allowed me to send an invitation, but they were highly skeptical that anyone would come."

About 2 A.M. on the morning of the special day, Bertsche was awakened by a tapping on his front veranda door. He got up and opened the door. The scene was bathed with light from a full moon. Out front he saw a worn, mud-splattered Landrover; in the shadows of the veranda he recognized the tall, slender silhouette of Pastor Kazadi.

"I'm sorry to trouble you at a bad time like this," Kazadi said. "We started out yesterday morning. The roads are terribly bad. We had lots of trouble. We kept getting stuck in the mud. Had someone not helped us, we never would have arrived. But now we are here. We are tired and dirty. Can we find a place to sleep? There are five of us."

It was the first time since the rending events of 1960 that a Baluba church leader had returned to the AIMM field to make his appearance among those who had expelled the tribe. The respect Kazadi had for Archie overcame the qualms he had about the kind of reception he would encounter. Leaders who had been skeptical of his coming were now rousted from bed to arrange sleeping quarters for their guests.

Archie and Irma had arrived by plane the day before. After breakfast that morning they decided to go for a leisurely walk on the station compound they had built during the 1950s. Just up the grade from the guesthouse they recognized standing in the road ahead of them the delegation from South Kasai.

"We had no inkling that we would see those men there," Irma recalled later. "When we were involved in the rehabilitation program at Bakwanga, Kazadi was the counselor we had come to rely on. So many times he had helped us bridge communication gaps and smooth ruffled feathers. But at that time Kazadi refused to return to the AIMM field for even a visit. He feared for his life. Now here stood Kazadi and our South Kasai friends. We could hardly believe our eyes. We were simply overwhelmed by our feelings of love toward them."

"Ki-i-i-ya!" Lutonga exclaimed as he rushed toward them with open arms. "What a surprising thing! Have you come all the way here to see us?"

There was a joyous reunion on the spot, with a round of hugging and backslapping and weeping. When emotions subsided, Kazadi spoke:

"We did not come for nothing. I have come on behalf of my people in South Kasai to give you thanks for your help to us. We have no way of ever finishing our indebtedness to you. God alone can repay you."

Tables were prepared under a spreading mango tree. There was a big feast that day, and speech-making, and singing, and reminiscing. Archie was overwhelmed with a sense of unworthiness. AIMM missionaries had left their distant posts to come join the festivities. Kazadi and his friends had sacrificed so much to come. Still, Archie recalled, the church was split. While conversing with Kazadi that afternoon, he felt prompted to broach the subject.

"You've been telling people today that you are unable to finish your indebtedness to me."

"Yes. That's the way it is."

"In my heart I feel there is a debt you have to me which you can repay."

"What kind of debt?"

Lutonga weighed his response. It was strong medicine, but he believed his old friend could take it.

"How can I return to my home country and retire in happiness when I remember that part of the AIMM church is split off to itself, estranged from the mother who gave it birth and from her other children? Will it stay that way forever? That is the debt I want you to finish."

Kazadi was moved deeply. What Lutonga had said was more than an appeal; it was a commission. Before Kazadi left Kalonda station that evening, he went to see Missionary Bertsche and shared his feelings.

"In my heart, I would rejoice if you missionaries would help bring us together as children of the same mother again."

25

... Full Circle ...

ON JANUARY 11, 1972, about twenty AIMM Africans with light baggage pitched and bounced in the rear of a Tshikapa transport truck headed east toward the frontier of South Kasai. In exactly the same way thousands of fear-stricken refugees had made this 210-mile trip twelve years earlier, fleeing the tumultuous events which then were ripping the fabric of society to shreds. Now this group of Africans was traveling the same road, this time hoping to stitch some of the pieces back together again.

"They were stopping at Luluabourg overnight. On the following day a smaller number of Baluba refugee leaders from the Kalonji clan would join them. These delegates, forming one group, would proceed to Presbyterian retreat grounds on the shores of Lake Munkamba, that once strife-plagued area on the Baluba-Lulua frontier, to meet with a group of equal size representing the church headed by Pastor Kazadi. The purpose of the meeting was to effect reconciliation between the Ngalula-clan faction of the AIMM South Kasai church headed by Pastor Kazadi on the one hand, and the church of the traditional AIMM field with its ally, the Kalonji-clan faction of the South Kasai church on the other.

Metaphorically, leaders of the two groups had already traveled over much rough ground to reach this point. After the Grabers' farewell in May 1969, Kazadi's desire for rapprochement was communicated to the AIMM home office. In June 1971, AIMM home secretary Reuben Short visited the field and mediated an initial encounter of small delegations from each group which met at Luluabourg. Both groups

231

wanted to define factors separating them and to seek ways of reducing these factors. Also, Short proposed a plan by which the AIMM home board could provide financial help to the Baluba refugee church program.

Following upon a recommendation from this first encounter, a commission met on November 17, 1971, to lay plans for a conference with larger representation, where factions might hopefully put aside their differences and be reconciled. It proved a turbulent meeting; long-harbored hurts were verbalized. Notwithstanding, members established necessary procedures for the conference and set its dates for January 13–15, 1972.

Now, larger representations from the church factions were gathering in conference to make the culminating effort toward reconciliation. During their layover at Luluabourg, members of the AIMM delegation met to consolidate their position. One recalled the unceremonious way in which the small AIMM delegation seeking reconciliation had been arrested and expulsed from South Kasai. Another suspected that the real motive of the Kazadi group for reconciliation was to start getting money from the AIMM home board. Hostile undercurrents on both sides still ran bitter and strong.

The AIMM group arrived at the conference grounds late that night. Delegates from both sides first met at breakfast the following morning. They exchanged polite greetings. Then the conference convened with forty delegates, including four missionaries. The first item on the agenda was to choose a moderator. Of three nominees, Pastor Kazadi won by a comfortable margin. To the missionaries, this was remarkable. Kazadi was elected only because some AIMM delegates had voted for him over their own nominee. Obviously, the Holy Spirit, though unseen, was also present and taking active part.

Kazadi took his place. He proposed that they draw up an agenda. This led into a heated discussion concerning the purpose of the conference. A large number of delegates participated in carefully calculated parleying. From the missionaries' viewpoint, it seemed as if the delegates were all treading gingerly around a fused mine, hunting for a handle by which to defuse it before it exploded. The torrent of words appeared to contribute little to the proceedings, but Kazadi apparently felt that their talking had important cathartic value. Finally, toward noon, Kazadi stood to take his turn. He had patiently listened to them; now they would listen to him.

"When I first arrived down-country in the AIMM field as a child, I was known only as 'Kazadi Lukuna,' " he began. "It was there that I became known as 'Pastor Kazadi.' My love, for most of the years of my life, was planted down-country. Who can be happy to leave a place after working there for forty years? If I died today, people at Charlesville, Tshikapa, Nyanga, and Mukedi would all say, 'Pastor Kazadi has died.' People of South Kasai where I now live would only say, 'They're burying another refugee.'

"What happened in 1960 started a fire that raged completely out of anyone's control," he continued. "When those things happened, I was terribly surprised; I saw some of our AIMM Christians stirring up the fire. We lost everything we had down-country; we fled as refugees to South Kasai. What one of you here would want to carry all the responsibility I was carrying at that time? There's not one of us here who would want to give account for all that happened then. When I was setting up our own church, was I happy to be cut off from you? I longed with all my heart for a meeting such as this."

Missionaries present were encouraged. Kazadi clearly was rising to the occasion.

"When a fire stops burning, and smoke subsides, and eyes stop hurting, people begin hunting for ways to repair things," the old pastor continued. "Everyone knows the great work Missionary Lutonga did for us when we were starving refugees in South Kasai. When I heard he was about to go home to retire, and they were having a farewell meeting for him and his wife at Tshikapa, I said, 'I must go in the name of my people and tell him how indebted we are to him.' When I talked to him alone at that meeting, he said I had a debt with him that I must finish. I asked him to explain what he meant. He asked me, 'How long will the children of one mother be broken apart? When will the quarreling and fighting end? When are you going to do like Jesus said and start showing love one for the other?' "

He had complete control now. Delegates hung on his every word.

"We are here to finish that debt. President Mobutu has brought an end to wars between tribes; he seeks unity for our country. All the countries of Africa are striving toward unity. It is time for us to again find unity in the church of Jesus Christ. Each of us has been speaking his mind about the purpose of this conference. In my thinking, its purpose is clear. It is to heal our divisions and to reestablish our friendship and oneness in Christ.''

His speech had commanded the respect of his black brethren. In a diplomatic but honest way, he had reminded AIMM delegates that powerful tribal elements among them had fed the fires of disorder, which had produced anarchy and had forced him and his people to flee. In those terrible days both sides had been guilty of non-Christian conduct. Reconciliation must be reached from both directions; and for his part, he was willing to forget the past and start building together again.

The assembly sat in silence, absorbing the impact of his words. Then Rev. Kabangy, general secretary of the AIMM church from Tshikapa, rose and spoke:

''We will all disappear from this earth. We will leave behind us our children, and for them, the church. What kind of church do we want to leave for them? It is also for their sakes that we must rebuild what has been destroyed, correct our mistakes, and heal our divisions. The purpose of this meeting will be to reconcile us again to our oneness in Christ.''

Kazadi asked all those who agreed to stand. The vote was unanimous. Someone said it was a good time to pray. Everyone bowed his head. Someone led in prayer. Then another. Then another. During those moments missionary delegates began to sense an amazing Power at work melting down barriers. One missionary choked up with joy. Another blew his nose vigorously. The tension which had prevailed a short time earlier dissipated and was supplanted by a sacred sense of unity in the Holy Spirit. After several had prayed, Kazadi adjourned the meeting for lunch.

Sessions of intense discussion were relieved by devotional periods and studies from church history. Then each of the groups brought its report of activities since the church's division. AIMM representatives were surprised to learn that the church group headed by Kazadi had fourteen ordained, salaried pastors, who ministered to 2,400 communicants. It had primary and secondary school systems comprising 218 classes and 7,199 pupils. It conducted a growing evening Bible institute program self-supported by the tuition of its 30 students, and it supported financially a network of resident village evangelists. The church had a comfortable operating budget, which had purchased among other things the large diesel transport truck that stood on the conference grounds, having brought the delegates. This measure of progress, without the help of foreign funds, tended to allay suspicions of the AIMM group that the underlying motive of Kazadi's group for reconciliation was to secure money. Consequently, attention began to turn toward the possibility of really working together.

Progress toward reconciliation was disrupted on the second morning, when a few aggressive younger men of the Kazadi group wanted to reopen debate on the purpose of the conference. They avoided stating their concern clearly. Kazadi, as moderator, listened patiently until it was clear that the fabric of unity so painstakingly woven on the day before was now unraveling, and tension was mounting. Then he took the situation in hand.

"My friends, I want you to first sit down," he said.

They reluctantly obeyed.

"We don't restrain anyone from talking at this conference," he explained. "Anyone can say whatever his heart desires. At the same time, the first day Pastor Kabangy and I both said that the purpose of this meeting is to put out the fires so that we can start building together again. You all stood to your feet, showing that you agreed. Yesterday we all sat for a sufficient period of time to hear your opinions. We must act like mature men who know how to pursue an objective we've set for ourselves. Since we agreed on what we want to achieve, we must ask ourselves: Are the words we speak now designed to keep on stirring the ashes so that fires stay alive, or do they work to help us put out the fires once and for all? Only if we speak words that fix things up are we worthy of discharging the debt we have."

Representatives from both sides spoke in turn, giving Kazadi their support. Then a neutral delegate rose to make a motion:

"We agree that, because of terrible events that happened in our country, we treated each other badly. But beginning today, we are forgiving each other of all those things and are leaving them behind us, and we will move into the future together."

The motion was adopted. The groups agreed that, while maintaining separate adminitrative structures, they would begin immediate collaboration in church activities. Discussion became animated.

"What will we do with the 'Short Plan'?"

"It talks too much about money. If we begin talking about those things now, it may ruin everything. The big thing now is to rebuild our spiritual unity."

"When can we meet again?"

"Whenever you want us to come see you," said a pastor of the Kazadi group, "you just let us know. We'll sweep our pennies together and find a way to pay the truck to get us there."

"Where should our next meeting be held?"

"Make it somewhere in the AIMM area," Pastor Kazadi said. "Let us drive up and down those roads in the land where we matured. When people see us there, gossip in their mouths about division will be finished."

The conference closed when delegates formed a large circle, held hands, and sang "Blest Be the Tie That Binds."

The next time they got together, it was in the AIMM field — at Nyanga, the mission station in the heart of the Bampende tribe, seventy-five miles northwest of Tshikapa. The occasion was an all-Mennonite Zaire's pastors' conference held July 7–13, 1973. Kazadi joyously returned to visit the field he loved. And gossip about division was finished. From the villages along the road out of Tshikapa, people flagged him down for so many chicken dinners that he was two hours late arriving for the conference.

The day finally came when the groups could sit down and talk about money. Representatives from the home board, the AIMM national church, and the two tribal clan-groups of the Baluba church met June 10–13, 1974, at Tshikapa. They legally consummated their reconciliation by drafting and signing a formal document that recognized the group headed by Kazadi as a legal entity and spelled out procedures for reinforcing spiritual union and for mutual collaboration in the sharing of resources.

And so Kazadi finished his debt. He knew there were still a few dissidents who sought to fulfill their personal ambitions. But all the groups of the church were fellowshiping together again; and practically everybody wanted it that way.

Pastor Kazadi returned to sit at peace in the land of his forefathers. He remembered when he had first arrived there as a refugee and had sat in the midst of the devastation of famine and war. He had asked himself then how such brokenness of his people could ever be healed. Now he

Refugee church leaders reassemble at Bakwanga; Matthew Kazadi is second from left. *(AIMM)*

Formalizing the reconciliation of the two church groups in June 1974: (from left) Levi Keidel, Matthew Kazadi, and Elmer Neufeld. *(AIMM)*

Archie Graber and Matthew Kazadi: Reconcilers

meditated on his long experience with Lutonga, and slowly the answer took shape. Brokenness will never fix itself. It can only be fixed by people. First, one must love those who are broken so much that he is willing to lay down his life to help them. Then he must work hard, on and on, his heart never weakening, until God shows a way to put the broken pieces back together again.

Archie Graber settled for retirement near Stryker, Ohio, the rural community where he had been reared. Often his thoughts returned to dwell on the church and its estranged brethren in the land now known as Zaire. Then one day a periodical arriving in the mail brought good news.

"I read the report of that Munkamba reconciliation meeting and just about jumped up off my chair," he recalls.

"Irma, I can hardly believe it," he said. "The way things were so torn up; the way people suffered and died; then all that bitterness and division. It is all finally finished. And to think that we had a part in putting everything right again. All our weeping and praying and weariness — it wasn't for nothing. Things have come out all right."

"Archie," she responded, "you used to feel so down on yourself because you had so few talents to give to the Lord. I used to get discouraged because things seemed so hard. I guess we just have to go where the Lord wants us to go, and be faithful with whatever we have even if it is hard; then we can know that the Lord will take care of the rest."

Irma was right. Through all his years in Africa, he never felt that he was doing anything extraordinary. Unwittingly, his faithfulness had been an essential ingredient in creating momentous events. He was reminded again of an incident which had occurred when he was a small schoolboy. One day he was in the woodshed of an elderly neighbor. He watched the stooped old man take a small hand ax and painstakingly chip the bark off a crooked oak limb. Then he saw the man cut a post from it and set the post with a crossbar in the backyard of his beautiful home to support his clothesline. The old man could have cut a nice tree out of his timber, but for some reason, he chose to use the crooked post.

"Like I've said so many times," Archie replied, "I don't know why the Lord chooses like He does; but if He can use a crooked stick like me, He can use anybody."